11-1-63

(63-8430)

spaces

Beatrice Webb's American Diary

1898

BEATRICE WEBB'S AMERICAN DIARY

1898

Edited by

DAVID A. SHANNON

THE UNIVERSITY OF WISCONSIN PRESS

Madison, 1963

Published by
The University of Wisconsin Press
430 Sterling Court, Madison 6, Wisconsin

Copyright © 1963 by the
Regents of the University of Wisconsin

Printed in the United States of America by
Vail-Ballou Press, Inc., Binghamton, New York

Library of Congress Catalog Card Number 63–8436

Contents

22660

Introduction

Beatrice Potter Webb's previously published diaries are an important source for the study of British social and political history. This volume from her diary, hitherto unpublished, contains material useful for an understanding of the American past as well as further clues to the diarist's character and social thought.

Beatrice Potter was born January 2, 1858, the eighth of nine daughters of Richard and Laurencina Heyworth Potter. The only son, younger than Beatrice, died when a small child. It was a distinctly upper-class Victorian home. Richard Potter was a wealthy capitalist with investments in various enterprises. For ten years he was president of the Grand Trunk Railway of Canada. Sickly as a child, Beatrice had almost no formal education. However, except for never developing a better than barely legible hand, her lack of schooling was no serious handicap as an adult because her father and his friends had given her a splendid education informally. The person closest to her outside the family was Herbert Spencer.

If she can be said to have had a teacher, it was he. Although Spencer was thirty-eight years older than Beatrice, from her early childhood she and the Darwinist philosopher were good friends. He arranged for her to become his literary executor, which arrangement he changed, of course, when she married the socialist, Sidney Webb. However, she apparently never embraced Spencer's individualistic, *laissez-faire* philosophy.

Beatrice's mother died in 1882, and her older sisters having married, Beatrice took charge of the operation of the home and became her father's hostess and confidante. She learned a great deal from him during these years about the operations of business. He became paralyzed in late 1885, and for the balance of his life she spent a great part of each year caring for him, a task she shared with her married sisters.

During the weeks away from her father she began her training as a social scientist or, she called herself, "an investigator of social institutions." She helped her cousin Charles Booth in the investigations of the condition of London's poor that resulted in Booth's monumental eighteen-volume *The Life and Labour of the People of London.* As an assistant to Booth she learned to interview well and acquired some knowledge of the historian's and statistician's methods. She also set to work independently on her first book, *The Cooperative Movement* (1891).

It was through her study of economic cooperation that in January, 1890, she first met Sidney Webb. Webb, already a socialist and a leader of the Fabian Society, quickly fell in love with the attractive and intelligent young researcher. (Beatrice in 1883–84 might have become the third Mrs. Joseph Chamberlain, but despite their mutual attraction she could not abide his principles and they did not marry. If they had married, she would have been Neville Chamberlain's stepmother.) A few months later they agreed to collaborate on a book about trade-unionism, and in the summer of 1891 the seminar-like courtship became a formal engagement.

However, the couple feared an announcement of her intention to marry a socialist would have an unfortunate effect upon her capitalist father, and they kept the engagement a secret from everyone but a few friends. Richard Potter died on New Year's Day of 1892, and the couple married in July.

Sidney Webb's background was startlingly different from his wife's. His father was an accountant, his mother a shopkeeper. Sidney had a bit of Cockney in his speech. He attended schools in Germany and Switzerland but left regular school at age fifteen to go to work as a clerk. Eighteen months younger than Beatrice, he had gone into the Civil Service and risen quickly. In 1881 he moved into the First Division of the Civil Service and went to work in the Colonial Office. Of superior intelligence, intellectually orderly, efficient, and extremely industrious, Sidney Webb clearly could have had a distinguished career in government. But in 1891, before his engagement, he resigned to pursue another career as a Fabian socialist and journalist. Beatrice's inheritance enabled them to live in comfort and devote full time to their work.

Their first project, other than the affairs of the Fabian Society, which Webb, George Bernard Shaw, Sydney Olivier, and Graham Wallas in effect directed, was a major study of the history and philosophy of trade unionism. They made an unusually efficient and thorough research and writing team. They wrote their first volume and saw it through press in less than eighteen months. In characteristic no-nonsense fashion, they started the book on Christmas Eve of 1892; it appeared as *The History of Trade Unionism* on May 1, 1894. The volume on trade-union philosophy, *Industrial Democracy*, appeared a little over three years later. The volumes were among the first major studies of trade-unionism in the English language.

Before embarking upon their ambitious study of local government—*English Local Government* was published in fifteen volumes—they undertook a trip around the English-speaking world, to the United States, on to New Zealand and

Australia, and back home again. Upon their return to London they pitched headlong into their many projects: the London School of Economics, the reorganization of the University of London, their study of local government, the Fabian activities, politics, and poor law administration among others. They rather rapidly became intellectual and political figures of national and international importance. Clearly, they and their Fabian friends were a major influence in Great Britain, the Commonwealth, and the Western world generally.

The Webbs' trip to the United States was not the first trip to the North American republic for either of them. In the fall of 1873, when Beatrice was fifteen, she had accompanied her father on a business trip to America. Also in the party were her second oldest sister, Kate, and her third oldest sister's husband, Arthur Playne. In the first published volume of her diary, *My Apprenticeship* (1926), she described her visit to Chicago, Yosemite, San Francisco, and Salt Lake City. As a tourist she found the trip "delightful" until she became seriously ill on the train from the West back to Chicago. Her father and his friend George Pullman, the paternalistic manufacturer of railroad sleeping cars, took her from the train in Chicago in a semi-conscious state. The western landscape, the San Francisco Chinese, and Mormon polygamy seem to have impressed her more than anything else in the United States. Sidney and his friend Edward R. Pease, in whose rooms the Fabian Society was founded in January, 1884, made a three-month trip to Canada and the United States in the fall of 1888. They traveled only as far west as Chicago and as far south as Richmond. Sidney did not publish comments on this visit, but Pease recorded a half-century later that they thought the United States in 1888 was "a generation behind Europe."

There is much in Beatrice's diary that helps toward an understanding of the American national experience. One of the Webbs' main subjects for investigation was the problems of American cities, particularly the governmental problems.

American academic historians have only relatively recently begun to become interested in urban history to a significant extent, and the entries in this diary by both Webbs are of use on that subject. Each of them offered descriptions and analyses of municipal government in the United States, Sidney usually in well conceived essays, Beatrice usually in a more discursive and sometimes gossipy fashion.

The Webbs sought out and interviewed a number of people who were prominent, or later became prominent, in American affairs. They had the foresight to interview two future Presidents of the United States—Theodore Roosevelt and Woodrow Wilson—when each was still relatively unknown. Beatrice's descriptions and impressions of Roosevelt and Wilson, as well as of John Peter Altgeld, Jane Addams, Lillian Wald, Seth Low, "Czar" Reed, and scores of professors are of value precisely because she brought an informed and intelligent mind from outside America to focus on her subject. Granted that Robert Burns has been quoted to the point of nausea, still the desire to see ourselves as others see us is widespread; and travelers' accounts give us that power. When the travelers were as perceptive as Beatrice and Sidney Webb, their accounts are of considerable value.

For the most part, Mrs. Webb restricted herself to descriptions of America and comparisons, sometimes unconscious, to Great Britain. But occasionally she offered some generalizations about the United States. Some of these generalizations were commonplace, made by many another English or European visitor. Some she would not have made had she known America better. But she had some insights that were ahead of her time. In her comments upon the shallowness of many of the "good government" reformers and her understanding of the basic reasons for municipal corruptionists being able to maintain political power she anticipated some of the work of Lincoln Steffens, who began his investigations of American cities in the decade after the Webbs' visit. Nor did Americans share her fear of the potentially "autocratic power of public-spirited and expert bureaucrats" at the time of her visit. Not until the rise of such vast organizations as the Central Intelligence Agency and the Atomic Energy Commission did many Americans see the danger to democracy in the well intentioned and expert bureaucrat. Americans today might well ponder her contention that if there should arise a civil service of experts in fields in which the public is largely ignorant, "it will become the most powerful and untrammelled bureaucracy in the world."

But Mrs. Webb, as readers of this diary who know America well surely will see, had her limitations. This uncut diary reveals much about its author. It reveals her as too provincial to understand or appreciate much of what she saw abroad. So British was she that she was quite incapable of understanding non-Britons. Thus, although she tended to judge American politicians by their intellectual powers or lack of them, she quite consistently judged American intellectuals by nonintellectual standards, primarily by their appearance and manners as compared to their British counterparts. Her comments about her host at Cornell University, Professor Jeremiah W. Jenks, are a case in point. She was aware of her prejudices: "It is perhaps difficult with English prejudices to be fair to such a man in such a position." Yet, even with that awareness, she wondered if it would not have been better if he had stayed in the small-town store in which he had worked as a young man. Jenks's lower middle-class and semirural manners and appearance obscured for Mrs. Webb the fact that he was rapidly becoming one of America's eminent economists.

Had the Webbs done more reading in preparation for their American visit, they would have profited from the trip more than they did. They quite obviously intended to investigate American government, particularly local government, but their previous reading on the subject, or at least what there is in the record about their reading, was scanty. They were familiar with Bryce's *American Commonwealth* and Wilson's

Congressional Government, but they apparently had no familiarity with the work of Frank Johnson Goodnow, later a president of the Johns Hopkins University, who had published two solid studies of American municipal government before the Webbs visited the United States. Mrs. Webb did not record that they had made an effort to talk with Goodnow when they visited Columbia University, where he was then a professor of administrative law, although they met several other Columbia professors.

One wonders, too, why the Webbs did not interview trade-unionists during their American trip. They had only recently completed a major study of English unionism. Characteristically, they were so immersed in their next study, of local government, that their previous work interested them not at all. The investigation of local government amounted almost to an obsession. In Washington during the war crisis of 1898 Beatrice Webb complained that it was an "unfortunate time to be at Washington" because "all the politicians to whom we have introductions are completely absorbed in Cuba." Without such unique singleness of purpose the Webbs would have learned more from their exertions.

On the whole, it is justifiable to conclude that Mrs. Webb learned a great deal about the United States but next to nothing from it—because she believed fundamentally there was nothing to be learned from the American experience. In 1911, when the Webbs made another trip around the world to visit Japan, China, and India, they crossed America via Canada and did not even venture south of the border to see what changes had occurred in the previous thirteen years. That she was a superior person is clear. But she was also insular because she was keenly aware of her superiority. She is reported to have said once, when asked if she had ever felt shy, "Oh, no. If I ever felt inclined to be scared going into a room full of people I would say to myself, 'You're the cleverest member of one of the cleverest families in the cleverest class of the cleverest nation of the world, so what have you got to

be frightened of?'" Such assurance stunted her potential
stature.

Beatrice Potter began to keep a diary regularly during her
first trip to the United States in 1873. She maintained the
practice for the rest of her life. She died in 1943. In 1926 she
published an autobiographical volume, *My Apprenticeship*,
in which she quoted at length from the diary. Sometime before 1936 she had a secretary reduce the scrawl of her hand-
written entries during the American visit of 1898 to a type-
written copy. She then went over the typescript, filled in the
words that the typist had been unable to decipher, and
changed some of the phrasing, spelling, and punctuation.
Immediately after publication of *My Apprenticeship*, Mrs.
Webb began a second volume of autobiography and diary
extracts. She had in her manuscript a chapter entitled
"Round the English-speaking World," which included her
1898 trip to the United States. The press of other matters,
however, prevented Mrs. Webb from completing the project.
Five years after her death, Barbara Drake and Margaret Cole,
who had published a perceptive biography of Mrs. Webb in
1945, edited the manuscript and saw it through press as *Our
Partnership*. They omitted the chapter on the 1898 journey.
Mrs. Cole subsequently edited and published two other volumes of the diary, bringing the story down to 1932. In 1959
a New Zealand publisher brought out the portion of the diary
that pertained to the Webbs' visit to his country.

I have reproduced the diary as Mrs. Webb left it after she
amended the typescript, keeping her punctuation and spelling except where obvious slips in writing or typing interfere
with the sense. A little more than two pages of quotations
from various of the *Federalist Papers* that she included at the
end of her "Superficial Notes on American Characteristics"
have been omitted, since the quotations had no special rele-
vance to her remarks. In order to prevent confusion, I have
added in brackets the correct spelling of names when she
wrote them incorrectly, as well as adding Christian names
when she omitted them. Similarly, I have added in brackets

the names of people whom she identified but did not name, mostly municipal officials. None of the material in brackets is from Mrs. Webb's pen. The portions of the diary reproduced in a slightly different type face from that of most of the volume are entries that Sidney Webb wrote. At the back of the volume is a biographical directory of most of the people mentioned in the diary to provide the reader with a little additional information. The starred footnotes are Mrs. Webb's; the numbered notes are the editor's.

The original and the typescript of the diary are in the Passfield papers at the British Library of Political and Economic Science, London School of Economics, and readers may consult them upon application to the chairman of the Passfield Trust. This volume represents volumes 17, 18, and the first ten pages of 19 of the typescript. All letters quoted in this volume are also in the Passfield papers.

Even for a volume as small as the present one an editor puts himself into the debt of others. I want to acknowledge the help of and express my gratitude to Mr. C. G. Allen, Senior Assistant Librarian of the British Library of Political and Economic Science, who was generous of his time and trouble and very helpful indeed; Sir Alexander Carr-Saunders, K.B.E., chairman of the Passfield Trust, who granted me permission to read, photocopy, and reproduce the diary and certain of Beatrice and Sidney Webb's letters; Sir George Lowthian Trevelyan, Bart., who permitted me to quote from certain letters of his father, Charles Philips Trevelyan; my friend and colleague, Professor John F. C. Harrison, who in several conversations illuminated my thinking about the Webbs and the Fabian Society; Mr. Irwin Klibaner, Mr. Donald J. Murphy, and Mr. Keith W. Olson, my research assistants, who were helpful in many ways; and the Research Committee of the Graduate School of the University of Wisconsin, which made a grant available to me that made the research in London possible.

DAVID A. SHANNON

July, 1962

Beatrice Webb's American Diary

1898

part **I** *March 29–May 29*

Our first journey round the world 1898

❨[*March 29th Mid-Atlantic 1898*

"**T**o America, Australia and New Zealand, when they might go to Russia, India and China: What taste! Just what one would expect from them" remarked a Tory acquaintance to a friend of ours.

A little group of Fabians came to see us off at Euston—Edward Pease, [George Bernard] Shaw and the [Graham] Wallas's. Bob Trevelyan came to see the last of his brother; Kate Courtney of her sister; whilst F. W. Hirst divided his attentions between C. P. T. [Charles Philips Trevelyan] and "the Webbs." We were a jolly little party as we steamed out of the station, all thoroughly satisfied with ourselves. Sydney Olivier sent to Washington on Colonial office business (to adjust the tariff with America for West Indian produce). He was burdened with C.O. papers and Blue Books and lent a certain official gravity to our tourist air. At Liverpool we were met by R. D. Holt and Betty and Sir H. Bacon (who mildly deprecated his anxiety to see Sidney). Our brother-in-law was in high feather. "Come along and look at your cabin:

3

you will see what an advantage it is to be connected with the
commercial aristocracy. The White Star Line have treated
you as well as a duke: could not have done better if you had
been H.R.H. himself. Come along, come along, this way:
we'll show them, Betty, what we have done for them." . . .
"Now what do you say to this?" and he led us into a charmingly fitted Deck Cabin—"You can keep your own cabinet
downstairs as well if you like. Now you see what it is to have
capitalist connections" chaffed Robert as we tried to inter-
polate words of appreciation and thanks.*

In spite of our gorgeous deck cabin the next three days
were solidly wretched. Sidney became a wreck from sickness,
C. P. T. and I struggled to keep up appearances but felt continuous inward misgivings; Olivier alone survived unscathed;
eat sumptuous repasts and worked straight on at his sugar
bounty calculations and at his "Play." In more lucid intervals
I investigated the careers of the Ship's Passengers—for the
most part a dull lot—commercial travellers (a deadly dull
type unless you can get them to talk their own "shop" which
they seldom will) prevailing and giving the tone to the
company.

Hebblethwaite is a railway engineer—Yorkshireman by
birth, settled for the last ten years in a Brazilian province—
Amazonas—1,000 miles up the Amazon. He has built a
small railway 13 miles in length (now floated as a Company),
lives in a town (Manaos) of 40,000 inhabitants. He has been
nominated as Governor of the State by both political parties,
but being English born cannot serve. A tall gaunt Yorkshireman with blue eyes, ruddy hair and moustache, irregular
features and pleasant expression, he has an agreeable awk-
wardness of gait and manner: otherwise is just the ordinary
energetic Englishman who goes out to organise other coun-
tries. "Don't you sometimes regret England?" I ask as we

---

* We afterwards gathered from a letter from Robert that we owed our
privilege not to his intervention but to the courtesy of Mr. Ismay who had
been much shocked by the attack on me by his son-in-law Geoffrey Drage
in the XIX Century a year or two ago.

pace the Deck. "Not on the whole; you see it is better to be a Boss in a small place than a nonentity in a great country. When I go to London or even Yorkshire I am lost. I look up an old acquaintance or two—but otherwise I know no one and no one knows me. London is like one vast desert to me. But in Brazil, out of the forty thousand inhabitants, thirty-nine thousand know my name! Everyone above a mere labourer speaks to me if I meet him in the street. Then the feeling of space and fresh air—up at five o'clock and riding all day. Then again the homeliness of the life: I can leave my horse standing in a street for six hours off hand and there it will be when I return. All human relations are familiar; every person knows every other person and all that concerns them." "But your evenings—don't they hang heavily?" "Not so," he answers: "every evening I have six persons to dine with me: the engineer and assistant engineer of the Electrical Light Station; the general manager of the Railway and his wife—a pleasant Portuguese woman—and then my little daughter's governess who does my housekeeping—another Portuguese woman. We four men play a game of whist and the two ladies discuss the day's marketing and the servants, and then we are all in bed by ten o'clock. Altogether life passes pleasantly."

"I am preparing a revolution too" he goes on—"I want to make Amazonas and the neighbouring State with its sea-board an independent Republic so as to get rid of the import duties which the Federal Government pocket in return for some useless soldiers they quarter on us at Manaos. Of course the revolution (he adds with a twinkle in his eyes) is somewhat in the future. I have got hold of everyone in Amazonas, but we must have a seaboard. When I get back I shall go down into the other State and get hold of people there: then when all is ready we will declare ourselves an independant Republic—every inhabitant who cares will become an *Amazonian,* and I can therefore be President. I only want money to do it. *Power is a mere matter of money* out there." "I thought," I interject "there was a wide suffrage in Brazil and a regular constitution for each State?" "Oh yes! of course. We have a governor and a vice-governor and a Congress—all elected by ballot. But no one counts the votes: or rather both parties declare the results differently. On one occasion there were two governors: the Congress declared elected by the two rival parties, and each governor met his congress and formed a cabinet. But the old government carried the day because it had the keys of the Treasury. You see a government is never turned out because it always declares that its nominees are elected and there is nothing more to be said. If you want to change a government you must have a 'Revolution.' You must organise a scrimmage in the streets and get hold forcibly of the Treasury. No one pays any attention to the voting: though it goes on just the same at appointed intervals. Democracy out there is a most amusing farce! Force of character with money can do anything."

Then he suddenly turned the tables and began with unselfconscious directness to cross examine me as to my opinions, political and religious. Somewhat taken aback I found myself describing the work of the Fabian Society—drawing it as big as he had drawn his influence in Amazonas. "But what do Socialists believe: what do they want?" "Ah" I parried, "our faith and our programme are far too complicated to be described in a few sentences after dinner. In England Democracy is not a farce: it is the most intricate of businesses: some would say the most elaborate of sciences: it would take me two hours' lecture at least to give you the A.B.C." "Can conceive no greater pleasure than to hear you lecture for two hours" retorts the Yorkshireman with awkward gallantry. "You said you lecture sometimes at the English Women's colleges: I'll send my little girl to college then perhaps she'll hear you lecture" he adds with a certain gentleness. "I must go back to Amazonas and become President of my New Republic! When I'm fixed up you can come out and witness from the President's palace *"The Farce of Democracy."*

B. is an American business man—(I gather trader in some speciality) with the clear cut well-lined face that would, in an Englishman, imply intelligence and acuteness. But a little conversation draws out the extreme conventionality of the man's ideas: his acuteness is a sort of quick adaptability to the most superficial circumstances. "The worst of America is that the Government is always meddling: cutting the business man down to do his work in a particular way. I don't want any one minding *my* business: I just want a free hand to go ahead in the way I think best." He was against income tax as "confiscation and unconstitutional," against silver; in favour of Protection; against all attempt to check the syndicates and trusts. Above all he was dead against a "Committee." "The German Syndicate to which my firm is Agent proposed that we should have a Committee to look after us. No Committee for me. I told them I haven't time to consult men who know less than I do myself; if I want suggestions I go to my own agents who have practical acquaintance with the details of the business; but these suggestions seldom amount to much. A business must be conducted by one brain and one brain only to be successful" dogmatically asserted the typical American business man.

❨*Westminster Hotel.* Disembarked Wednesday morning (30th).

Sydney Olivier went off to Wall Street to consult sugar merchants, C. P. T. and Sidney journeyed out presenting introductions and I unpacked. In the evening we went to the theatre: acting more refined and more amateurish than the English stage.

❨*March 31st.* Lunched with John Graham Brooks to meet Seth Low and [William S.] Rainsford. J. G. B. is an old acquaintance of Sidney's—a former Unitarian minister in Massachusetts. He left the ministry (presumably became agnostic), became a casual lecturer at American Universities, acted also as a government commissioner in foreign parts on special investigations. Endowed with small independent means he lives at the Century Club New York, whilst his family are mostly abroad. Always on the look out for the newest development—equipped with diversified culture. He spotted Sidney and the Fabians ten years ago as the newest thing in politics, and without being one of us he has always been our friend. A pleasant, courteous, interested man—a dilettante of the best sort. Perhaps it is because he seems to have no ties that he is not a person whom one much respects or looks up to. He has not "placed himself" in the world—he has drifted—though always into good channels.

A bright little private compartment in a French restaurant, a delicious little lunch, culminating in ice cream, coffee and cigarettes—the brilliant mid-day sun streaming in—were the pleasant circumstances of this meeting with President Low. He is a strong built stout man—with an intelligent kindly face, rugged features and pleasant dignified manners. No self-consciousness or pretention, looks and acts like an English country gentleman or well-bred business man. But he expresses himself remarkably well and states his arguments and facts with admirable precision and lucidity. One feels that he would understand anything one said, he would ignore no "point," and give it the right answer from his own intellectually consistent point of view. He has plenty of humour of the friendly sort. By temperament he is a practical opportunist—he is in fact far less of the superior person than I foresaw. More than this I cannot say on first sight. He gave us a most interesting sketch of the constitutional development of New York City ending in the great charter of last year which he, as one of the commissioners, helped to draft. I did not master with sufficient clearness the details to transcribe this rapid sketch. But one point was evident: the constant and increasing distrust of the American—whether he be a superior person or the man in the street—of an assembly of representatives. Any device to escape being ruled by a representative assembly seems acceptable: a referendum, a nominated body, or a dictator, a closely knit syndicate ruled by a boss, even Tammany itself—so long as you escape government by representative institutions. Tammany is government by a firm of contractors, who are given the job of governing the city for so many years by the electors and who quite naturally govern it entirely through their own men. But Seth Low, though he recognised that the American distrust of the representative body was itself proof that American democracy was less developed and efficient than that of England, accepted this distrust as inevitable and had helped to carry the feeling into effect in the new charter of Greater New York, which adds to the power of the mayor and his officials and detracts from that of the municipal assembly. On the whole he was hopeful: "We have got rid of the most open form of theft in our city corporation, and the standard of public integrity is steadily rising. The nation has only just realised that the great problem before it is city government: we have been concerned with slavery, with the reconstruction of the United States, and a thousand other issues of immense importance; but now we are settling down face to face with this complicated problem of how to organise life in our great cities—and we shall solve the problem with the same rough and ready success as we have solved the others."

⟨*April 1st.* We lunched to-day with President Low at Columbia University. This University is an old foundation, formerly King's College, dating from George II. Until the last twenty years it has been considered, by the older foundations of Harvard and Yale, a secondrate concern fitted only for the New York commercial classes. Latterly it has sprung ahead both in membership and status. The group of unfinished buildings stand in a fine position at the extreme end of New York, overlooking the Hudson and Riverside Park. In outward form this cluster of buildings resembles something between a hospital and the London polytechnic: inside there is lavishness of expenditure on all that is utilitarian and a complete absence of charm—an absence so striking that at times it almost gives the impression of squalor. Seedy-looking young men come in and out:—the "smartest" and best set up inmates being unquestionably the girl clerks who abound in the basement addressing circulars and adding up figures. The heating and lighting apparatus is the finest of its appointments—the library, class and lecture rooms are thoroughly convenient and well thought-out—the laboratories seem to me somewhat poor. There is a spacious gymnasium and swimming bath which perhaps contributes to its polytechnic air and reminds one irresistibly of the People's Palace in Mile End. The various professors are much more like the professors of a German Realschule than the tutors of an English university. But I rather doubt from the individuals I talked to whether their lack of breeding and culture is compensated for, as in the case of the Germans, by thorough going specialism. There, again, they seem to me more like the teachers of a London polytechnic or of the evening classes of a provincial town, or to the masters of higher grade board schools. In these surroundings President Low stands out as a great personage. He is a wealthy man and has made the University, over which he presides, his "hobby." Obviously he is an admirable organiser—a first class business man softened and refined by public spirit and real interest in university subjects. But he also shows little of the distinction so manifestly wanting in professors, students, and buildings.

"A very bright man," "a man of great influence in the country" were the epithets applied to Dr. Albert Shaw by various of our friends. As almost every other individual in America is a "very bright man" or "a man of great influence in the country" we did not attach too much importance to this recommendation. We were agreeably disappointed. Dr. Shaw has even a certain charm. He is not physically prepossessing: a tall slip of a man—sloping shoulders, small head, low forehead, bad teeth and commonplace manners. Neither is he entertaining. In his desire to be helpful he spares you nothing; his words flow evenly on, no short cuts, or flashes of humour; a plain recital of facts. But the delightful absence of all selfconsciousness, of all vanity, the naive desire to get at the truth, the unremitting energy, the gentle disposition and general kindliness lend a certain moral dignity and grace to his personality. He is a shrewd observer, a man whom it would be difficult to deceive. He has a clear intelligence, though his occupation as an editor and journalist has made this intelligence superficial even if it ever had greater possibilities. At present he edits the *Review of Reviews* and is one of the strongest personalities in the Good Government Party. He comes from Ohio and began life at Minneapolis.

He gave us much information first as to the persons we ought to see in our enquiry into American municipal institutions, secondly as to the political machine of New York City and New York State. The State is practically in two divisions, New York City and the rural districts with Buffalo as an industrial centre and Albany as the capital. The two parts differ entirely in character. The rural districts are puritanical in spirit, limited in outlook, with agriculture as the chief occupation. New York State is metropolitan if not cosmopolitan, with a strong Irish and German element both alike intensely hostile to the puritanical spirit of the native American. To the German who has come away from Berlin or Frankfurt because he has too little personal freedom in his homeland, the sabbatarian temperence proclivities of the rural American seem intolerable. He came for more freedom from personal supervision, not for less. To the Irish Catholic the strict evangelical desire for an orderly and self-controlled life is a reminder of the hated English dominion at home. On the other hand, to the old established families of New York State the influx of these "free livers"—these intellectually anarchic Germans and the morally anarchic Irish—is anathema. There is thus a moral issue—an hostility of assumptions dividing New York City from the rural districts of New York State. On these conflicting views of social expediency the two great party machines rear themselves: Tammany standing up for personal freedom from vexatious restrictions, and the Republican Party asserting its ideal of moral righteousness. Hence the ordinary citizen, who is also a good party man, believes himself to be supporting a moral principle whether he is a German or Irishman in New York, or a native American in a village in New York State. But though the professional politicians of both parties pander to these sentiments or principles, the party machine goes grinding on without any real regard for them. In both cases the party machine carries into political life, the commercial maxim of each man for himself, guided by the motive of pecuniary self-interest. Exactly as the economist of 1850 held that business enterprise ought to assume that each man would follow his own pecuniary self-interest, so the politician in America believes that public administration should proceed on the same assumption. But as one man can do little or nothing in democratic politics, those who wish to control public administration in their own interests must combine in a corporation—i.e. a political party which will aim at exploiting the public just as the manufacturing corporation does. This exploitation must not be carried too far; Tammany must keep within certain limits in its exploitation exactly like a bank or a capitalist syndicate. But there is one striking distinction between political and commercial profitmaking. The two great party machines are in collusion against the ordinary citizen: they recognise that they are each the only alternative to the other and that so long as they can both consent to any given act of dishonest government, there is not much to fear. Thus

[Richard] Croker (the head of Tammany) and [Thomas C.] Platt (the head of the Republican machine which dominates New York State) are always conspiring together and with the great capitalist corporations who find the funds of the two political corporations. The Albany state legislature is the market place for these higglings between the two parties; they are perpetually selling concessions to each other without it coming to the knowledge of the ordinary citizen. This supremacy of the state legislature over the local life of New York City on the one hand, and of the rural districts on the other, is wholly bad. Through Platt's power Croker is able to cheat his democratic constituents in respect of the affairs of New York City; through the help of Croker, Platt robs the republican citizen of New York State. Such is Albert Shaw's statement of the present state of affairs as far as I remember it.

Lobbying or the buying of members individually has now been largely superseded by regular subscriptions from capitalist corporations to the funds of the party in power or likely to get into power. In New York State both machines are kept in full efficiency since one controls New York City and the other the Albany legislature.

Note the American contempt for the vested interests or "established expectations" of the individual citizen. Private enterprise is permitted to trample on the individual; to shut off the light of his house, disturb him by noises, or even to kill him by carelessness, without exciting any particular public objection.

⟨[*Washington, April 6th.* Diplomatic gallery 9.30: waiting till 12 for President's message about Cuba.

An unfortunate time to be at Washington, seeing that all the politicians to whom we have introductions are completely absorbed in Cuba.

Sidney and Trevelyan spent the first day presenting introductions to the British Embassy, to Carrol D. Wright, Roose-

velt etc., and yesterday we hung about the lobby of the
senate sending in our cards to various senators to whom we
had letters. Went over congressional library and made friends
with superintendent. Trevelyan called out Senator [Henry
Cabot] Lodge and introduced us, and he and Sidney proceeded to cross examine the senator as to working of the
senate, and the position of chairman of committees. But
Senator Lodge gave mere "book" answers and though he invited Trevelyan to his house showed no sign of wishing to
see us again!

In afternoon went to tea with Miss [Emily] Tuckerman.
The Tuckermans are an old and wealthy family with a charming house. The family consists of an elderly lady and an attractive woman about 35, exquisitely dressed and with delightful voice and manners—obviously they keep a political
salon. We met there Theodore Roosevelt (with whom Sidney
and C. P. T. had already talked) the most remarkable man I
have yet met in America. Theodore Roosevelt is a short thick-
set, bullet-headed man with an extraordinarily expressive
face, all his features moving when he speaks. The dark,
shaggy eyebrows, the keen grey eyes and the powerful jaw—
all combine in a series of grimaces as he gesticulates his
words. He has abundance of ready wit, splendid fighting
courage and a thorough knowledge of the world he lives in.
Perhaps it is the deliberately sought out rough and tumble of
his past life that has lent to his outward address a slight
vulgarity. He has the loudness and hearty egotism of the man
who has shouldered his way through life. For though he belongs to one of the old Knickerbocker families of New York
and has had large means from boyhood, he has preferred to
fight in the ring—as a pioneer ranchman in Dakota and for
many years as a professional politician inside the republican
machine. "My difficulty" he said "has been to live down to
my ideas not to live up to them: I have often been thwarted
in my desire to carry out certain measures by the fastidious-
ness of my conscience. And I have always regretted it."

In graphic language he described his first entry into political life. Directly he left Harvard he determined, both from motives of public spirit and of curiosity to get inside the machine of his party. He put himself down for the nearest republican primary in New York. "They rather liked the idea of a Roosevelt joining them" he added with an expressive twinkle. He found the club a mixed lot. Some respectable artisans and lower middle-class men, others disreputable saloon keepers. "I insisted on taking part in all the discussions. Some of them sneered at my black coat and a tall hat. But I made them understand that I should come dressed as I chose. 'If you come in your shirts I don't care a damn; and if I choose to come in a speckled coat I shall do it.' Then after the discussions I used to play poker and smoke with them. I was neither afraid of them nor did I patronise them. Presumably I got a following; they thought me a good fighter and liked the fun. At that time the club was run by the Jews and the Irish resented it, and one of the local bosses—John Murray—ran me against the sitting member for the state legislature."

Then followed a vivid description of John Murray—his personal integrity, his crude democracy and his strong partisanship. "The idea that you should not reward your political comrades by office and that there should be any educational test for office was abhorrent to Murray. Not to insist on the spoils when you got into office and share them equitably among your political allies seemed almost as dishonorable as not to pay your private debts. And yet personally he was one of the most honest fellows and would not have touched a penny himself."

Roosevelt's career in the Albany Assembly seems to have been somewhat unsatisfactory. "I never could get on with the big bosses—Platt and others. With the local bosses I managed well enough: they were flattered by being treated as fellow-beings by what they conceived to be a reputable man; but Platt was too big a person for that: he only resented my independence. *And I soon found out one political truth. If you want to have influence inside the party you must sacrifice your independence outside.* You won't be listened to in party counsels, if after the question has been discussed and decided, you go and vote according to your conscience in the assembly. Political life is a constant compromise between inside influence and public adhesion to your own principles. That's what dear good people like Miss Tuckerman and a mad-man like Jack [John Jay] Chapman don't understand."

I could discover in Roosevelt no particular political views except jingoism, or, as he would say "national responsibility" towards the world, civil service reforms, and "good government" generally—with a strong bias towards individualism.

12 o'clock.

The Senate is now full—each man in his place. The Vice-President [Garret A.] Hobart—a common looking man (political placeman) is sitting in the chair: an old clerk with an ugly voice is going through the routine business—the little pages (political appointments for four years) are dashing about carrying petitions from Senators to the table. Platt, the boss of the New York State, sits to the extreme left—a mean looking dissenting-grocer sort of man; [Matthew S.] Quay, Boss of Pennsylvania—a real low sort, mean, and cunning, dissipation writ large on his face; [Marcus Alonzo] Hanna, a typical capitalist—railway king type, far superior to the other two bosses. [William B.] Allison, Chairman of Finance Committee, a Roman senator with American business shrewdness added to his dignity. Prevailing type: elderly man of character and intelligence.

1 o'clock.

Dreary process—the clerk reading through the detailed "appropriations" in various departments, including, for instance, the paint and nails used in keeping up the Washington Monument! Apparently we are waiting until the U.S.A. Government hears by cable that the American consul has got away from Havana. [Sir Julian] Pauncefote (English Ambassador) has just come into the crowded gallery—Olivier offered his place in duty bound—but His Excellency refused and left the gallery with his daughter, making room for the French Ambassador's wife. Overheard from an attaché that Great Britain has insisted on U.S.A. having free play and squashed any intervention from European Powers in Spain's favour.

A sell! We were cleared out of the galleries for "executive business" and when we returned on hearing that the "session was open" the doorkeeper of the senate (a friend of ours) sent word that there would be no "Message"—a fact we might have inferred from the non-return of all the diplomatists.

Went to dine with Carrol D. Wright, head of Federal Labour Bureau. A tall military looking man—like the colonel of a line regiment—An honest and industrious public servant, but muddled-headed: does not inspire one with confidence in his manipulation of statistical data. Seems submerged in his facts. His household was distinctly middle-class, a dowdy little wife, a bright but insignificant daughter—an old mother, black servants. Dinner 6.30, soup rather badly cooked, foreshoulder of lamb, and the inevitable ice-cream and coffee. Lester Ward and his wife at dinner; the first a somewhat noted sociologist, former disciple of Herbert Spencer, now a collectivist. Should have thought him a dreadful old bore if he had not been collectivist in thought! But I pricked up my ears when I heard him assert he always preferred to travel by a railway which was in the hands of an official receiver! and that his thirty years experience of the American civil service made him conclude that this old theory that private property was necessary to efficiency was a fallacy; that in fact, the government secured the best efforts from a man. Both he and Carrol Wright were optimistic about America, and specially insisted on the improved character of the American civil service.

Tea at the British Embassy. Sir J. Pauncefote a heavy sensible honorable Englishman, his wife a chronic invalid, his daughters commonplace women of no occupation—quite harmless and pleasant. The room swarmed with well-dressed tall young fellow countrymen—some were attachés and others young touring aristocrats staying there.

When we returned to the Hotel we were told that the Speaker's private secretary was awaiting us. Sidney looked for a smart young man but found a sort of middle-aged Presbyterian deacon. The Speaker [Thomas B. "Czar" Reed] would see us at his hotel 9 o'clock that evening.

"He is just there by the lift" was the answer of the hotel clerk. And there stood a large heavy man with sloping shoulders, unwieldy body and a large head somewhat pointed towards the top, with immense development of jaw and chin, synchronising with the equally disproportionate development of the lower parts of the trunk. To look at he was a cross between Charles Bradlaugh and [John T. W.] Mitchell (of the Co-operative Wholesale Society); clean shaven, with long upper lip, expressive mouth and shrewd green eyes. He inclined his head as we presented ourselves, and, with a joking word to the young girl who stepped out of the lift, motioned us in. Up we went to about the fifth storey: he led us along a passage, fumbled for a key and opened the door into a slip of an office with two rocking chairs—a large one for himself opposite a writing table, a smaller one for a visitor. The walls were bare except for an advertiser's almanac and a few little coloured pictures cut out of illustrated newspapers and pinned to the wall—of children playing or of love making. The furniture consisted of the aforesaid rocking chairs and writing table, one or two straight backed chairs and a revolving bookcase filled with miscellaneous parliamentary papers books and reports. Sidney took the rocking chair and I settled myself in a straight backed chair. All this in perfect silence. "Excuse me, I must just look through this letter: it may need an answer." And he read the letter slowly through. Then he leant back in his chair and looked at us with calm attention, just as if he expected one of us to open the debate. Sidney with his bland manner described our interest in the procedure of the House and how the London County Council had modelled itself on the American Congress (!!) and had divided up into committees reporting to the House. And then he began to cross-examine the Speaker in deferential language. Mr. Reed responded with perfect frankness and a yankee drawl "Oh yes, I choose the Committees. And my dear sir a precious business it is too. It takes me a month's hard work. I don't look like a delicate man, but I took to my bed after I did it for the first time. So many considerations: the personal status of the members— their States—the interests they represent and their own personal qualifications and he added significantly, their personal disqualifications." "No" he responded to a question from me "I don't let the minority nominate their men on the committees. That's what they do in the Senate: the party caucus on each side nominates its own members. We don't allow that in the House. The Democratic candidate for the "Speakership" (the informal leader of the opposition it appears) came to me at the opening of the House and asked me to keep certain members of his party off certain committees. 'My dear fellow,' I answered, 'I can't indulge my own private hatreds and I am not going to indulge yours. And it is no use my beginning to make up the committees from *your* point of view; it is *my* business to make them up from my own party's point of view.'" "Yes," he answered Sidney, "the Chairman of Committees has a large control over its work. The first man named by me is a chairman, and he in his turn appoints sub-committees, and to these sub-committees he apportions the bills." "Does a bill referred to a committee by the House necessarily appear on its agenda?" Sidney asked. "No," drawled out the Speaker, "the Chairman decides to which sub-committee it goes." "And is there any written report from each sub-committee?" "No—that is to say very seldom—usually the chairman of the sub-committee reports personally to the committee." "And there is no printed report of the work of the full committee?" pressed Sidney. "No" reiterated the Speaker "we don't print much, it is all by word of mouth." At this moment there was a knock at the door. Mr. Reed opened it and there ensued an underbreath conversation between him and the man outside. "Oh it's *that* devil is it?" we heard the Speaker say, "I'll come down and talk to the lot of them: it's hell if they do that. I say, have you a good cigar over there?" (An interpolation which we surmised had something to do with keeping the House in order about Cuba—the Speaker being a "Peace" man). "At your service Mr. Webb" he courteously said when we offered to go, "there is plenty of time: delighted to answer any more questions. You were asking whether there is any approach to a cabinet among the chairmen of committees of the House of Representatives. I can answer that in the negative. We have, as you know, the Committee on Rules, of five members; myself, two members of the majority, and two of the minority. Practically it consists of the three majority members, who report their decision as to the conduct of public business to the other two. This committee determines the spheres of all the other committees and apportions the bills among them. But this committee is not made up of the principle chairmen and has no connection with them." "Is there any connection between the executive committee of the Republican caucus and the Chairmen of Committees of the House of Representatives? Do they meet and discuss what line shall be taken?" I ventured to ask. "So far as I know" drawled the Speaker, "we have no executive committee of the Republican Party in the House of Representatives. We have the congressional committee prior to an election; but just at present I rather fancy that that body is non-existant; at least I never hear of its meetings. No, we have no 'Party Committee' for the House of Representatives. In America, Mrs. Webb, one man thinks himself as good as another and rather better too; we don't like committees taking matters out of the hands of the members." "And yet you give tremendous powers to individuals?" "That's another matter: if a man has inspired confidence, we trust him, but not a committee. With a committee the ordinary man does not know which one he is trusting and who is responsible for the policy."

We then diverged to the question of the "order of business" and expressed our surprise that two members should be allowed to be on their feet at one time. "I follow the drift of the conversation between them" casually remarked the Speaker. "Of course, you English keep better order in your assemblies; but an American assembly would not stand your strict rulings; I wish they would; we should get through the business far better." Then we suggested that it seemed to us strange that a private member might increase any item of the appropriations in the third reading. "You have hit on our weak point, my dear sir, the Treasury has no protection. Any fool or knave can get more money voted for any object. I have been looking round for some way of stopping it. The difficulty is that the Senate does it; our fellows would not give up the privilege while the Senators had it. Moreover, your English plan of ministers proposing the estimates would not apply as we have no parliamentary ministers." Sidney suggested L.C.C. [London County Council] method of only permitting private members to refer any proposal for increase of expenditure to the committee concerned. The Speaker's face brightened and he seemed struck with the idea.

From the procedure of the House we turned on to the two financial scandals—the Pensions and the River and Harbour Appropriations. The Speaker explained that about 1884 a Democrat had proposed that all pensions granted for service in war should be payable from the date of injury. "That completely altered the situation, and without our knowing it. Up to that year many who could have claimed pensions did not care to ask for six dollars a month. But when their claim appeared to them as a lump sum of "arrears" say 6,000 dollars, then it was a different matter and they succumbed to the Claim Agent. When we voted for it we thought it meant an additional nine millions, which with our surplus of forty millions a year seemed a mere bagatelle. As a matter of fact it has run into millions and is always increasing. It is a beastly business. We ought not to have done it: but the Republicans thought that if they refused they would be 'slaughtered.' I voted for it," added the Speaker in a tone of penitence.

"The Rivers and Harbours Committee, that is another beastly mess. Here we have been voting millions for the improvement of the navigation of the Mississippi for years past and all we have really done has been to add to the acreage of local landlords by embanking their lands. But you see it is a scramble: every State seeks to rob the Federal Government and there is a tacit conspiracy between all sections and all parties. I am always turning the matter over in my head to find a way out of it" drawled the Speaker with puzzled thoughtful expression. "We treat our corporations worse than you do" asserted the Speaker, "the ordinary member will not understand that corporations are *only a way of doing business:* he imagines them to be mysterious beasts with claws and a cloven foot."

Finally he poured scorn on the publications of the Agricultural, Census and Education Departments. "Waste of public money: I say. Now just look at this stuff" he added, lifting out of his revolving bookcase the bulky census return. "Who wants to know all this stuff: it's never any good to anyone and it's obsolete before it's published. If I had my way I'd clear the whole lot of these departments out of the way— pure waste of public money" he reiterated, "and no-one the penny the wiser for all this miscellaneous information."

Here ended our interview. Speaker Reed is a strong man, with consummate knowledge of the men and the situations

of American political life. He is a rule of thumb man, desti-
tute of any kind of culture, and therefore with little capacity
for suggesting alternative and better methods of doing public
business. But he is upright, (within the limits of party war-
fare), public spirited and deliciously unselfconscious, and
endowed with a fine stock of primitive humour. He is completely absorbed in getting through the work of government
as efficiently as possible. But because he lacks all culture, he
lacks any standard of excellence. His success and his failure
are the obvious results of great natural capacity, without
knowledge of men and affairs outside his own immediate
personal experience.

I gathered that if he has any political ideas he accepts the
intellectual traditions of the ordinary American business man
—a naive individualism tempered by an opportunist consideration for any new forces that may appear. I compared him,
in looks, to Charles Bradlaugh; but he has none of Charles
Bradlaugh's self-consciousness and vanity, and neither has he
Bradlaugh's undoubted intellect. He is a man with great experience but with no ideas and no capacity for them—an
ideal philistine.

《*April 8th.*
Lunched at American Restaurant with Roosevelt and
friends. Roosevelt deliciously racy: told stories of his life on
a western ranch whenever he could tear his attention off the
Cuban question. But most of the time he was breathing forth
blood and thunder. "B (a senator) came up to me and said
that he was in favour of going to war but did not agree with
my reasons. Go to war because you don't like God, if you
please, but *go to war.*" Altogether the lunch with the war
party did not impress me with the sobriety of the American
statesmen. And the way in which accusations of stock ex-
change corruptions, as motives for peace or war, are being
bandied about, is not edifying!

([April 9th.

Knocked up with cold. Sidney and C. P. T. interviewing Congressmen: come back full of scorn for the House of Representatives, especially for leading Democrats: still more for Populists. Impressed by some of the Senators. They gather that the business of the Committees is done in the most informal way: sometimes the committee consult together on the floor of the House, or the chairman goes round and gets the various members to affix their names to a bill that he is furthering. No proper minutes are taken, only notes which do not carry conclusive authority. Constantly go back on resolutions if they have been passed in the absence of some important member. With one Committee raising the revenue—largely for protective purposes—with all the others spending money according to specific and separate votes—it would be an extraordinary coincidence if there were any kind of settled relation between revenue and expenditure.

([April 10th.

Dined at the British Embassy last night: deadly dull. Interviewed Secretary [Lyman Judson] Gage, one of McKinley's Cabinet (Principal Secretary of the Treasury). According to this extraordinary American constitution he shares with the Chairman of the Ways and Means of the House of Representatives and the Chairman of the Finance Committee of the Senate, the task and responsibility of raising the revenue and paying the bills presented by the several Committees, in accordance with the appropriations of House and Senate.

He did not impress us. He is a superficially good-looking man—substantial in figure with regular aquiline features, broad forehead, large nose and fine beard. He is dressed like a smart bank cashier. Then you come to look into his face, stupidity or rather utter lack of any intellect is the dominant impression: his flesh is pasty and hangs heavily under his eyes and round about his nose. His mouth is disguised by his fine beard; his eyes are blue gray without any expression

whatsoever—they might just as well have been china eyes.
He speaks in slow measured tones, with that intolerable habit
of some Americans of sparing you no word—every sentence
being a dull paragraph out of the dullest and most elementary text books. He is obviously a representative of the mon-
eyed interests—a "sound man" (sound money man?) put in
by the banking interest. No sympathy and little knowledge
of men or institutions. I should imagine he would make a
fairly good cashier and has the ordinary enlightened view of
the desirability of some relation between revenue and expenditure. It was hopeless to talk to him, because he gave
mechanically mere book answers to all our enquiries and
gazed at us with a dull suspicion as we pressed home one
question or another. All the old commonplaces about sound
currency and free-contract and democratic institutions came
out syllable by syllable as if he were dictating them to a first
standard class in proper copybook form. He is said to be
pious; he may be honest: but he does not matter.

([*April 12th.*

WAR OR PEACE

Went yesterday to Diplomatic gallery of House of Representatives to hear President's message. The "House" is an
immense oblong hall—larger I think than either Queen's Hall
or St. James—with wide open galleries all round it—five
tiers deep. The body of the hall is arranged as an amphi-
theatre with seats and desks for all the members radiating
from the Speaker's Dais, with gangways between them leading to the numerous exits. Hence the largeness of the floor
space needed to seat the 350 members, with its endless opportunities for gossiping groups of members. When we arrived at 11.30, half an hour before the opening of the proceedings, the House was crowded in every part (except the
Diplomatic Gallery—apparently the Diplomats go to the
Senate). In the galleries there were some 1,200 persons: on

the floor of the House, shifting gatherings of representatives with their friends and relations surged up and down the gangways whilst little parties of men and women were sitting informally on the seats and desks. Everybody in the House —some 2,500 persons—was talking so that the din of voices was deafening. The gay easter hats of the younger women and the running to and fro of the children gave the look of a fancy bazaar or a mart of respectable shop-keeping folk. Presently a young clerk steps on to the Speaker's dais and in sonorous voice cries: "Ladies and gentlemen, I have to ask all persons, not entitled to the privilege of the floor of the House, to immediately retire." This announcement makes small difference to the chattering crowd. However, five minutes before twelve o'clock the friends and relations file up the gangways and one lady after another steps out into the corridors. Some twenty children—mostly little girls—remain firmly seated, either on their fathers' laps, or on the neighbouring chairs of absent members. One little girl, I notice, is corresponding in deaf and dumb language with friends in the gallery throughout the morning's proceedings. At 12 o'clock the Speaker lets fall the hammer: there is silence: the members rise in their seats and the chaplain improvises, in impressive tones, a prayer suited to the occasion. But directly the prayer is ended the chattering in galleries and on the floor begins again, whilst a clerk gabbles through the clause of a bill. The Speaker is chatting to a friend, but every now and again he rises and in his good humoured but dictatorial tones cries "The House will be in order," and for two or three seconds the House and galleries are silent, only to begin again in subdued tones which gradually acquire their normal volume of sound in every man's attempt to be heard above the din. The disorder is good-natured and quite ready to be called to order, but equally ready to revert to its natural state of disorder. At a quarter past twelve a seedy looking old gentleman appears in one of the gangways with a large folio of paper under his arm. "Mr. Speaker" and there is a lull in

the House and all turn round to look at him "A message from
the President of the United States." All members resume
their seats and there is dead silence while an elderly clerk
reads slowly the long-winded epistle from the Speaker's dais.
For over half an hour the crowd listen patiently without a
sign of approval or disapproval. Whether it is the enigmatical
character of the message with its historical precedents and
balanced arguments, or whether it is the spirit of orderliness
and decorum, there is no mark of enthusiasm or disapproval
from the members. After the clerk has finished the oration,
[Joseph W.] Bailey, the leader of the Democrats, asks for the
correspondence relating to the subject; the clerk reads a
second message from the President laying the correspondence
before the House. Then a Republican—Chairman of the
Foreign Relations Committee—jumps up and proposes that
it be referred to the Foreign Relations Committee for consideration. Passed unanimously and the House returns to its
routine business and becomes again a chattering multitude.

When we return, in the afternoon, we find the scene
changed. The Speaker's chair is occupied by a common-
looking individual who is chatting to a couple of friends. The
space between the Speaker's dais and the desks and seats of
the members is filled with a little crowd of about 30 members.
A large sheet—which at first we mistake for a blackboard has
been fixed to the back of the clerks' table so that all the House
may have it in full view. In front of this expanse of paper
stands a young fellow with striking features and long wild
hair—his coat sleeves somewhat turned up so that he can use
his arms and hands more freely. He is roaring at the top of
his voice, swinging his arms about in a wild fashion, now
pointing to the printed sheet, now doubling his fists as if he
were preparing for a fight: close to him stands an imperturbable official reporter who is taking down his words. We
gather that the member addressing the House is presenting
the minority report from the election committee on an election petition which the House is now considering. The crowd

round him changes from time to time, just as the crowd does round a cheap-jack in the Mile End Road. Now and again some individual interrupts him with a question or a jeer. "God have pity on the people whose advocate you are" he retorts scornfully to a seedy looking young man who has been for sometime interrupting him. The galleries are still crowded, but the floor of the House is comparatively empty. Little groups of members talk together in various parts of the House; other members read their newspapers with their feet up on the nearest seat. The louder the young man roars, the more he gesticulates, the louder become the voices of the members who are conversing together and the stronger wax the undercurrents of continuous chatter in the public galleries. The Speaker's deputy obviously finds it now difficult to talk comfortably with his friends. He rises, and letting the hammer fall with tremendous force urges in shrill tones "The House will be in order; members will cease conversation." The remonstrance has little effect.

But the scene has again changed. The member addressing the House walks to his seat followed by the imperturbable reporter and one or two of the crowd. "I yield the floor to the member for Mass" he cries. Then in an opposite quarter of the House an elderly person rises and begins to orate on the iniquitous proceedings of the New York Republican party. A new reporter (apparently there are rapid relays of official reporters) comes and sits on the desk opposite to him with his back to the Speaker, and a fresh little crowd gathers in the nearest gangway. The old gentleman is a respectable sort of dissenting deacon and is full of righteous indignation. But he is constantly interrupted by questions, and his speeches rapidly degenerate into retort and repartee with the crowd who are listening to him, as to the political morality of New York. The Speaker's deputy is quite absorbed in his chat: and no one pays any attention to the proceedings except the orator and his little crowd of opponents. The young man who has yielded the floor of the House, having refreshed himself with a cup of tea brought into the House by a little boy, saunters up to the edge of the little knot of listeners so as to help his friend out by answering some of the questions. So the comedy goes on, shifting from one quarter of the House to another. Eventually the finding of the majority of the committee is carried by a large majority. Throughout the latter part of the proceedings Speaker Reed has been wandering about the House, sitting down beside different members and talking earnestly with them—all, by the way, on the republican side. Some of them we identify as chairmen of committees, so presumably he is arranging questions of policy.

(From the debate we gathered that the chairman of the committee which presents the report and the senior member of the minority of the committee have the time allotted between them and that each of them redistributes it among the members of his own party.)

([*April 13th.*
Again we spent the day in the House of Representatives. A report on a bill for a railway in the District of Columbia (a district administered by Congress) was presented by [Joseph W.] Babcock (Chairman of the Committee on D. of C.). He made an amusing speech, judging by the roars of laughter which rose from the little knot who were listening to him, and he and his little audience indulged in joking retorts and repartees as to "free trips" and "free refreshments" etc. The Speaker, who had vacated the chair (the House was in Committee of the Whole), joined the group and grinned broadly as he listened to the fun. Then Babcock sat down. Here seemed to end the business of the House. From this time until the end of the sitting, the members who were fortunate enough to secure time from Babcock and the leading Democrat, fired off speeches on every conceivable subject. When we returned from lunch we found an impassioned Irishman marching up and down the little space in front of the Speaker's dais, flinging his arms about, clenching

his fists, hammering the desks within his reach, and bellowing at the top of his broken voice about the "Great Heart of America demanding War." Then rose a thin acid looking young lawyer from Montana ([Charles S.] Hartman) who read out, with admirable delivery, an extremely clever squib purporting to be the Republican Platform of 1900—dealing with Cuba, the Gold Standard, the Dingley tariff and with a constant refrain of "our great and good master Marcus Aurelius Hanna" and "Money the master: everything else the servant." This was greeted with cheers and laughter by the Democratic side of the House; the Republicans refused to notice it and went on chatting in groups. Three quarters of an hour of the time of the H. of R. of a people on the eve of war was taken up by this parody of a hypothetical future document. A shady looking customer—J. H. Lewis of Washington State—next took his turn and poured out a diatribe against McKinley for usurping the title of "the Government" in his dispatches to Spain: "*We* are the Government" shouted the outraged Democrat "and we have not expressed our opinion on the tragic crisis." Then came the Republicans' turn. An elderly and respectable looking gentleman—[Ebenezer J.] Hill of Connecticut—rose in his seat and read in sober and deliberate tones an essay on the Gold Standard, a sort of Penny Encyclopaedia article on elementary economics (date about 1850) with all the old stuff about Abraham's tomb— buying the sepulchre for pieces of silver—and the Goldsmiths being the bankers of the middle ages—a description of a visit to the Bank of England and so on. As he read steadily on and refused to answer questions, some of the Democrats got angry and called for the Chairman's order as to whether this was really pertinent to the subject still before the House, namely, the Railway of the District of Columbia. But the Chairman refused to consider "the point of order"— a right decision on his part, seeing that the Democrats had been allowed to read their squibs and spout their rhetoric irrespective of its subject matter. Otherwise the old gentleman seemed to give as much satisfaction as the other speaker; he had about twenty of the more elderly members of his party listening, with open mouths, to his portentous commonplaces and at least ten of them insisted on shaking hands with him as he tied up his bundle of papers. About 4.30, after four hours of these interestingly irrelevant proceedings we began to weary and went down to the Democratic Lobby and sent in our card to Bailey, Leader of the Democrats.

Clean shaven, with large sensual features, long black oily hair and enormous expanse of white shirt finished off with white evening tie, Bailey, to English eyes, looks a cad of the worst description, a strange combination of a low class actor and rowdy stump orator. With familiar friendliness and unctuous tones he motioned us into a recess and enquired what he could do for us. We asked for some explanation of the day's proceedings. "Well, you see it is just as well to let them talk. We don't want them to pass laws; at least we democrats don't—we think that there are too many laws already and that most of them were better repealed. They must either legislate or talk, so we let them talk" said the "leader" of the democrats—the official position and the acknowledged leader of the party which claims to represent progressive ideas. "With your usual practical capacity" I smilingly observe "you manage remarkably well; you certainly attain your end with an almost artistic finish. But what meanwhile is the Committee on Foreign Relations * doing?" "Oh! that has been waiting till the Republican majority have settled their internal quarrels. It met yesterday afternoon at 4 o'clock; the Republicans adjourned it till 10 the next morning. Then when the Democrats came this morning, the Republicans again adjourned it till 12 o'clock; then again till 3 o'clock. I hear that this afternoon they presented their resolution and left the Democrats in the committee room to consider them. The committee will report to-morrow." "Do committees never meet

* This Committee was considering the President's message—virtually the declaration of war with Spain.

then?" I ask. "No important committee meets as a whole" answered Bailey. "For instance, the Committee of Ways and Means which prepared the new tariff never considered the tariff. The Republicans took weeks to manufacture it, then laid it before us—I was a member of the committee—and gave us exactly 24 hours to consider it before the committee reported it to the House."

With fraternal greetings to the leader of the party of Progress we left the House.

《[*April 16th.* Missed witnessing the "free fight" in the House of Representatives by going to the Senate.

《[*April 18th.*

From first to last, so far as I can make out, there has been no debate in the House of Representatives on the Cuban resolutions. These resolutions, drawn up in secret by the majority members of the Foreign Relations Committee, were carried through the House without permitting, either the peace at any price party, or the official opposition—the Democratic party—to make any objections or propose any amendments. This was accomplished by the extraordinary procedure—which seems customary—of closing all opposition by the introducer moving the "previous question" at the end of his speech so that no more can be said. Very naturally the pent up feelings of the silenced minority found relief in a free fight on the floor of the House. What with reading each bill, clause by clause, talking at large on any conceivable subject with no resolution before the House, the absence of any agenda or order of business, and the silencing of debate on all vital or urgent questions, the proceedings of the House of Representatives are so extravagantly absurd that one feels as if one were looking at a comic opera—a malicious travesty of American institutions to please an aristocratic audience.

As we shall not go again to either House or Senate I give a few general impressions. The public sessions of the House of Representatives resemble the meetings in Hyde Park with a difference; the speeches to little groups of "passers by" are not delivered simultaneously but successively. But I do not think it would make any difference to the efficiency of the House if they were delivered simultaneously: all that would be needed would be a few more official reporters. The one object of these public sessions seems to be to secure a report of the speeches of individual members in the *Congressional Record* to be circulated among the respective constituents. This purpose would be obtained by simultaneous speeches; time would be saved and a larger number of members would be able to satisfy their electoral needs. Only members of the party to which the Speaker belongs make any pretence of listening to the oration unless indeed a few of the other side join the circle in order to heckle and disturb. If both sides spoke simultaneously these disturbances would be avoided for such members as care for listening to these tirades would always have a man of their own party to listen to.

There is a considerable variety of type among the members of the House of Representatives. Among the Republicans there are quite a number of respectable "go to meeting" looking men, professional and business men—mostly traders and lawyers; these shade off, through the better class professional politicians (who conduct the business of politician much as they would conduct their shops—on perfectly well-understood principles of pecuniary self-interest) to the sensual dissipated looking individual who, in England, you would put down as a bookmaker or a disreputable publican. The Democratic party are a ramshackle lot—heavy slouching men with long hair and big moustaches—a type unknown in England—ci-devant workmen with rough clothes and awkward manner, undeveloped young men with narrow chests, low foreheads, red ties—what we should call "S.D.F." [Social Democratic Federation] youths—whose occupation in the House seems to be heckling and disturbing the speaker of the other side. Lastly, among the Democrats are a certain number of enthusiasts and cranks—who, whatever the subject to be discussed, fire off their crude theories and economic heresies whenever they get a chance. Towering over the motley multitude is the figure of Speaker Reed commanding no respect but inspiring a certain fear in the common run of members and treated with obsequiousness by members of his own party. From watching the House and Mr. Reed's relation to it, no one would gather that he cared for its honour or its efficiency. One could almost imagine that his intention was to let the House degrade itself in order that he might have less resistance to his will. To him the House is merely a circumstance like any other circumstance to be overcome or circumvented in the interests of the party. He is in no sense the guardian of the House or its protector or leader: he is simply its shrewd and forceful manipulator. I imagine under his rule the House will lose the remnant of its power and become more and more dominated by its committees—or rather by the majority members of these committees. As, however, the revolutionary elements in the House seem, with every election, to be strengthened, the mere machine officials being replaced by the foolish enthusiast or the shady crank, we may look for a good deal of disorderly anarchy as a reaction to the increasing autocracy of the Speaker. If I were an American I should feel utterly despondent about the future of the House of Representatives. With abominable procedure —procedure which would disgrace an International Socialist Congress(!)—with no self-respect, with little intellectual leadership, with a predominantly loose moral character—it seems doomed to impotence varied by disorder. Its only redeeming characteristic is the easy going American temper —that strange mixture of shallowness of sentiment and shrewdness of intellect—which enables a gathering of Americans to pull itself together and accept with goodwill the decisions of the majority or discover some compromise which saves the situation from becoming disaster. One wonders sometimes whether they are not laughing up their sleeve at

our naiveté in imagining that they are doing more than playing at government and getting well-paid for it into the bar-
gain.

~The Senate is an entirely different body. Here there is a
body of corporate tradition which obviates the necessity of
much formal procedure. There are many notable faces among
the senators—large headed fine featured men with grave and
dignified manners; almost punctilious in their behaviour. On
the Republican side the business men and successful lawyers
predominate with now and again a low looking boss carefully
dressed and with quiet manners. On the Democratic side
there are some interesting looking individuals—handsome
foreign looking men from the South and the West—a type
that seems to be purely American. But we have not been impressed with any attribute of the Senate other than its appearance and manners. We have heard the best speakers: they all
fire off speeches which deal with the entire subject in general terms and which do not attempt to debate, to answer
opponents arguments or offer new points for discussion. And
the speeches are constantly degenerating into empty rhetoric;
they abound in quotations from well-known authors or from
their *own* former speeches. It is true that there are few personalities and that American Senators are more polite than
our English parliamentarians. But one is inclined to think
that the absence of personalities is large occasioned by lack
of ready wit, by lack of *actuality* in their political intelligence. And the methods of transacting business are almost as
stupid as those of the House. Every bill is read through by
the clerk; there is no closure and there is a constant chatter in
the galleries and on the floor of the House—above all there
is a sense of unreality—of powerlessness—as if the Senate
were a "show" body whose main function is to look dignified
and impressive so as to remove from the mind of the American citizen the sense of humiliation which might have been
produced by a visit to the House of Representatives.

The question always rising in our minds was who governs

the U.S.A.? The so-called "Cabinet" is made up of the head clerks of the various departments—head clerks who have not the advantage of being permanent officials. The President unless he is an unusually strong personality, is checked at every step by the constitution, and has no one to rely on as advisers and executive officers. The House of Representatives is powerless owing to its procedure and to the poor quality of its membership. The Senate is an apparently strong body; but even here there is a feeling that the majority of its members are kept in the dark. We are inclined to think that the deciding voice, in the present government of the country, is a group of men, including the Speaker, his lieutenants (the Chairman of one or two Committees of the House) and a certain group in the Senate including the bosses of the Republican machine—Hanna, Platt, Quay and [Stephen B. Elkins] Elkin and [Arthur P.] Gorman, the boss of the Democratic machine, together with some of the chairmen of the senate committees, e.g. Alison, Chairman of the finance committee. At any rate it is this group who seem to dominate the present administration. McKinley, we gather, is an upright man but made of putty, taking impressions from the stronger men around him. Perhaps of all the recognised parties of the constitution, the Senate representing as it does great wealth, and the Heads of the machines of both parties has the largest measure of independence. But there is no responsible government, no body of men who can be held accountable or whom the electors can control. And there is always a hidden and irresponsible authority and power which shifts from group to group according to the personalities that crop up in the constituent parts of the constitution, written and unwritten.

Sidney is always asking whether there is any advantage to-day in the federal form of government. We gathered that the authority of the separate state legislatures is steadily declining; the American citizens are limiting the power of these bodies by elaborating checks on their activities and by shortening their sessions. Meanwhile the federal congress is relieved from any consciousness of its responsibility for solving actual problems by the existence of the state legislatures; whilst the municipalities are constantly being thwarted and distorted by the political exigencies of the two political parties in the state legislatures. Exactly as there seems in the constitution of the U.S.A. to be no organic connection between the elector and representative or between the executive and the civil service, so there seems to be no organic relation between central and local authorities. In all these cases organic connection is replaced by power to obstruct.

❬*April 20th.*

Interviewed [William Torrey] Harris, head of the Bureau of Education—one of the Departments that Reed sneered at. He was formerly Superintendent of the St. Louis schools. He believed in elected School Boards, (the tendency being now to let the Mayor appoint Commissioners), and proposed that the members should be elected by small districts with a residential qualification. He gave as his reason that the little man who got elected in his own ward—usually a well-intentioned person without extraordinary ability—could contradict the mischievous libels of the newspapers and could explain to his neighbours and constituency the work of the Superintendent. In Harris's view the representative should represent and explain the Civil Service in the constituency; he should not control or direct the Civil Service according to the desires of his constituency, seeing that the ordinary elector had no policy. Harris was an excellent elderly gentleman—essentially an "elementary" or "Sunday school" teacher type—with a taste for writing fluffy pamphlets on "social evolution." He had no desire to raise the standard of education. He was an essentially worthy man, as worthy and upright as Carrol D. Wright—only instead of C. D. W.'s muddle-headed eclecticism, Harris had the egotistical dogmatism of the self-made man who had painfully educated himself without contact with superior brains.

We have made friends with Worthington C. Ford, Head of

the Treasury Bureau of Statistics. Another most worthy individual. An alert industrious cultivated person, with a
private income and social position—belonging to the Mug
Wumps. Brought up on the "Nation" and "Evening Post"—
a professional statistician and an amateur historian. He is
an Anglo-maniac and despises American institutions. Took
greatly to us and did his best to enlighten us as to the iniqui-
ties of the machine. Is a free-trader, a "gold standard" and a
peace man; McKinley's government did not care to remove
him partly because of his efficiency at office work, partly because of his social connections. These officials of the intelligence departments of the government—all permanent, perhaps because of the character of their work—seem to me the
most upright and independent part of the government servants. But they are all living in back-waters; they are left undisturbed because no-one cares much what they do or how they
are doing it. Possibly they form the nucleus of a new kind of
civil service, made up of university men with a love of their
work and an expert knowledge of it. If ever such a civil
service should arise in the United States and gain permanence of tenure, it will become the most powerful and un-
tramelled bureaucracy in the world. Once get permanence
of tenure and a high educational qualification and there is no
check in the machinery of American government to the autocratic power of public-spirited and expert bureaucrats. Perhaps a dim inkling of this is at the bottom of the popular objection to a permanent and trained civil service as "un-
American."

⟨[*April 21st.*
Visited two institutions—the Howard University for coloured folk and the new Catholic University. The Howard
University represents the philanthropic inclination of the
federal government, after the war, to raise the conditions of
the coloured population. It is a seedy survival; old-fashioned
in its educational methods, little else than mechanical drill-

ing in classics, mathematics and theology; and very inferior in staff and equipment. It reminded me somewhat of the institutions in London for the conversion of the Jews—except that its students were willing and even enthusiastic in their attempt to better themselves, many of them supporting themselves by manual labour. It was a pathetic sight to see these young men and women of all degrees of blackness (some of them coal black, with animal features, others quite white and refined looking, but with some hidden trait of the negro, forbidding them intercourse, on equal terms, with the surrounding population) gathered together to take part in a sniffling little religious service. They were all so anxious to learn their lessons, so docile and modest, so naively anxious not to be physically repulsive,—in a word so painfully conscious of their inferiority of race. In their wistful expressions —deprecating repulsion, one thought one could read past and future tragedies of feeling. And the intellectual chaff they were chewing would only impede their progress—unfit them for manual occupation and narrow, instead of widen, their outlook. Perhaps it was the half-conscious realisation of this that made the little pious New England minister (who taught them moral philosophy) so depressed and silent as he led us through this seedy and outworn institution.

The Catholic University was a complete contrast. Indeed, it seemed a little too "previous." Charmingly situated, admirably planned with a grace and charm in its interior, and a lavishness in its equipment, with wide awake and cultivated professors, and the most advanced methods: all it lacked was students! But the professors were a welcome relief from congressmen and senators; they were almost the first Americans we have met who were not "provincial." Some of our questions they did not care to answer, but they always understood them. They were so far more attractive as individuals than most Americans; they had depth and light in their eyes, they had warm feelings and acute intelligence—they had a sense of perspective; they knew how one part of life was related to the other. One got out of that wearisome groove of literal language and textbook knowledge into which one usually falls in talking to any American. They understood assumptions alternative to their own, and knew that there were alternative ways of carrying out common principles. If I were an American I should be tempted to persuade myself to become a catholic in order to enjoy the luxury of the freer and wider culture and intellectual comradeship brought about by the old tradition and wide relations of the catholic church throughout the world. Catholicism seems to give to the American the very qualities he most needs—reverence for authority and historical knowledge of human affairs, a consciousness of the inexplicableness of things, and a scepticism as to the validity of the banal assumptions of the commonplace mind.

Early yesterday morning, I wandered out for a last view of Washington. Brilliant sunshine and a deep blue Italian sky. The wide streets of shining asphalts, pavements for foot-passengers, street and foot-way lined with trees, so that each highway resolves itself into two or even three shady avenues; the charmingly laid out open spaces with the marble and bronze statues of American and European worthies rising out of green lawns and flowering shrubs and fruit trees—the beautiful public buildings—the absence of heavy business traffic, the smartly dressed American women, the picturesque coloured folk—all these circumstances give to Washington a bright gracefulness and simple dignity of its own. There is charm and self-restraint in the "White House" of the President, an English 18th century nobleman's country house, rising out of plain turf, with its iron gates flung open as if to indicate that any citizen might call and find the President at home and ready to receive him; there is impressiveness in the absolutely plain marble obelisk, which towers over the city, to commemorate the national hero—Washington; there is an extraordinary effectiveness in the way in which the beautiful buildings of the Capitol dominate the city and seems to be the culminating point of all its avenues. And yet Washington, with its purely mechanical arrangement of streets, with its perfect finish in the centre of the city, and its ragged and untidy suburbs of wooden shanties and dust-bin spaces, is strangely unsatisfying. You fail to discover, with longer acquaintance, any further charm; you are even disillusioned: for when you come to look into details there is shoddy execution and commonness of conception in the construction of its finest buildings. Here as elsewhere mechanical repetition and impatience of further thought characterises American civilisation.

¶[*Baltimore*

Mr. and Mrs. Buckler—an attractive young couple—she a young Englishwoman, he a cosmopolitan American settled in Baltimore—welcomed us warmly.[1] Met the City Solicitor [John E. Semmes] at lunch; he introduced us to the Mayor [William T. Malster]—a private client of his for the last twenty years, which accounts for the fact that though the mayor is republican the solicitor is a democrat.

The mayor was an immense man like some strange animal—a rhinoceros (?)—reminds one of a hugely inflated [Charles Thomson] Ritchie (President of the Board of Trade). He has been in office some months and says most of his time has been taken up in making the new appointments. He was returned by the action of the Mug Wumps who veered round to the Republicans in order to break the Democratic machine which had always ruled the city. (Why is a Mug Wump like a Ferry: because he spends his life in going from side to side). But he has disappointed the Mug Wumps by dismissing all the officials and appointing new ones. He told us that he could not avoid doing so because "the American is a practical man and will not go on working for his party and see other men grow old in office." Notices are up

1. Judging from the occupations of the few Bucklers in the 1898 Baltimore *City Directory*, this was probably William H. Buckler.

in all parts of the municipal building stating that the mayor would only see applicants for office between 10 o'clock and 3 *"because the business of the city must not be interfered with"*(!) A man of no education, he has had a remarkable career, having established a large shipbuilding concern with the handicap of borrowing capital at high rates of interest. I should imagine that within the limits of the rotten American municipal tradition, he tries to do his work with efficiency and honesty. We afterwards attended the meetings of both branches of the council. In both chambers the members were lounging in their seats smoking and dozing or reading newspapers, whilst the president and the clerk transacted the business. Procedure as childish as usual. No printed agenda, all resolutions and bills read word by word by the clerk. The council, considering itself a legislature and not an administrative body, reads all ordinances three times and has all sorts of mechanical checks to hasty legislation, which, of course, only operates when the party in power desires the business checked. Bad type of councillor—all ward politicians. The machines of both parties are at present in abeyance, the dominant republican party being split into sections. Each man is therefore for himself. In the present state of public morality there is no advantage to the community, in the absence of a machine and its boss. Though the corporations find this council as a whole more difficult to buy, there is more petty corruption and more inefficiency and blundering than when there is a well-organised machine, with a corporate consciousness of responsibility to the citizens and with a capable man as leader. The boss, who is seldom if ever a member of the council, makes it his business, not merely to "deal" with the large corporations in the interests of his party, but to take counsel with able business men as to how the financial affairs of the city can be best managed; he also vetoes any scandalous appointments. In the large number of transactions in which he cannot benefit his party by selling the interests of the city, he is an efficient, well-informed and comparatively long-sighted administrator, susceptible to public opinion and newspaper criticism.

In the evening a reception at President [Daniel Coit] Gilman's of John Hopkins' University. Dull couple, extremely conventional, but Gilman has, it is clear, organising capacity; he knows what is practicable in a middle class American town. John Hopkins University seems, however, to be hardly holding its place. We spent a day there; saw the professors of the political science and economics faculties and addressed the students. All the arrangements admirable: students rather superior looking young middle-class men; professors of commonplace American type except [Jacob H.] Hollander (Jewish extraction) who struck us as promising and with the understanding of a Jew. Dinner in the evening with Fabian Franklin (Jew) Editor of "Baltimore News"—again the Jewish intelligence—a relief after the literalness and conventionality of the American mind.

❨[*Philadelphia*

Staying with Talcott Williams, assistant editor of the "Press" the principle newspaper of Philadelphia. Agreeable house, with simple style of living and rough and ready service. He is an able cultivated American, a supporter of the machine (the principal proprietor and editor has just been appointed postmaster general in McKinley's government). The wife is a bright woman, straightforward—sensible, who has organised the reform party in her own ward. The house seems frequented by civic reformers, university professors and also by the better kind of politicians. Mr. Talcott Williams is an individualist, desires to minimise government and is therefore not specially keen on improving the calibre of the representative and the official.

The group of young men who constitute the economic and political science faculty of Philadelphia University appear far more alive and generally cultivated than the professors of Columbia or John Hopkins. They are not so common in appearance and manners, and they have more of the stock culture of the English university don. But there is a refreshing absence of any "side" or "affectation," a charming simplicity of personal life, and a genuine interest in public affairs. The women I have met in Philadelphia impress me favorably —they are sensible and public spirited—trying to put their hands to the plough and doing their utmost to raise the tone of public administration in all the ways open to them.

The city government is a hotbed of corruption, though according to Talcott Williams it is improving. The same constitutional features as Baltimore: two chambers, divorce of legislative and executive functions; powerful mayor and clique of salaried officials; councillors are not paid as in Baltimore, but all of them are ward politicians. The last scandal was the lease of the gasworks, a measure which was "bought" through both chambers—some of the members are being prosecuted for openly taking bribes. There is no party strife in the council—the republican party being overwhelmingly strong. But certain members are known to belong to this or that powerful corporation or to this or that boss. We attended a session of each chamber; the members were a low looking lot—All the same, these ward politicians have a certain distinction of physiognomy—they are forceful men: a strange combination of organising capacity, good fellowship, loose living, shrewdness and strong will. The corrupt municipal councillor in England is usually undistinguishable from any other ordinary man, if anything he is more commonplace, with less intelligence and less character than his fellows. In the U.S.A. he is a professional—with an expertness, a self-confidence and a strength of his own. Hence the appearance of these town councils is in a sense more distinguished than one would expect to see in an English town council noted for corrupt dealings; at once more distinguished and more degraded. The well-shaped head and prominent eyes, heavy jaws, self-confident and easy manner, ready tongue, make many of the ward politicians far more attractive and interesting species of parasites than the seedy little nondescript shame-faced persons who, in English Local Government happen to be open to corrupt influences.

There was no printed agenda in either chamber, and no audit of accounts. We interviewed the mayor [Charles F. Warwick]. For many years the city solicitor, he is a shrewd pleasant person, well versed in city government. He has worked hard to get a body of permanent officials. Against all "direct employment" he believes in all work being done by contractors in order "to keep it out of politics." This is clearly an honest conviction on his part and to some extent justifies his signing the gas lease. Without fine scruples, and tolerating with complacency the lower side of public life, he has the American desire for efficiency in executive work that saves American city government from absolute disaster. What constitutes dishonesty in public affairs is so much a matter of public opinion that where profitmaking out of city businessmen by elected representatives is taken for granted, men of far better abilities and far better character become its agents than in a country where pecuniary self-interest in city affairs is not openly tolerated. And as there are only certain occasions in the government of a city in which private gain is possible or practicable, the rest of the city affairs are managed with very fair ability and good conduct; quite as well, if not better, than they would be by honest but inexperienced reformers, without knowledge of men, or experience in the technique they have to direct.

From the genial mayor we passed on to the bureau of the director of public works. A large built imposing person— stupid and ignorant, but again with a certain executive energy. He described to us the whole mechanism of his department from his relation to the committees of the council to the way in which he gave out contracts. According to him there was no control exercised by the council's committee over his activities except cutting down "appropriations" for items, or passing stray "ordinances" about details in which particular members had a personal or political interest. If these resolutions were particularly objectionable he would go to the committee and remonstrate with them; in other cases he would try to get round the resolutions or under or over them. Like the mayor he wished to limit the power of the chambers to strictly legislative functions. "They often meddled with executive business" he complained. He altogether resented my suggestion that it would be better that the council should be made up of more distinguished men. "They were quite good enough, if they were more superior they would not know what their fellows wanted." He regretted the lease of the gas works. But he explained that what with the starving of the department, the constant cutting down of his proposed expenditure on new plant, on the one hand, and the ridiculous ordinances passed by the council as to the hours, pay and number of those to be employed on the other, it was impossible to work the department satisfactorily. "Why our clerks were only worked from 10 to 3 and we were forced to employ 20 men where only 10 were needed. The gas company has changed all that; no nonsense about hours; the clerks now have to work as long as they are wanted; no nonsense about there being two men to do one man's job. And how could the plant be kept in proper working order when my estimates were cut down by any committee-man who wanted to claim in his ward that he had saved the city 1,000 dollars!"

He explained to us in some detail the working of the civil service provision. He had got rid of the water engineer "who was not satisfactory to me." By the rules he was obliged to notify the civil service commissioners who publicly advertised the fact and appointed three eminent engineering experts (one was the leading professor at the university, the other two leading civil engineers) to conduct the examination. This examination resulted in five persons being selected from the candidates, out of which the city official might take his choice. "Would any Democrat be among the candidates?" I naively asked. "No Democrat would apply," answered the official with something as near a wink as the heavy stupidity of his countenance permitted. "And from the five you would take the man you thought the ablest?" I asked. *"The one who suited me best"* corrected the official with a certain dogged frankness.

Among the ordinances of the council was a "fair wages" resolution insisting that the council should employ no man for more than eight hours at less than one dollar 75 for the day. To this resolution both mayor and director of public works vehemently objected, both considering that it went far to make direct employment undesirable. No suggestion had been made to bind contractors to pay fair wages or work short hours, the mayor believing that if such resolutions were passed it would be disallowed by the supreme court of the state as an unconstitutional interference with freedom of contract. We came away with a mixed impression from the town hall. From what we saw the municipal bureaucracy was improving, becoming less influenced by politics and more expert in character. But the legislature was at once corrupt, inefficient and demagogic; able to check good officials in their enterprise, whilst utterly unable to control bad ones either in malversation or gross inefficiency. Talcott Williams was rather dismayed that we were not more favourably impressed. He maintains that American city government does more for its constituents than English city government and does not run them into debt. He instanced the supply of 180 gallons of water per head per day as contrasted to the 36 of London. We replied that every other person seemed to be recovering from typhoid fever! (The water is taken direct from the river) and that it was no economy and very bad book-keeping not to raise capital for what was capital expenditure. So far as we could gather this story of the gas supply was likely to be repeated in the case of the water. At present the water department is being starved; the loan of $3,000,000 needed to secure filtration being refused by the council. Meanwhile a syndicate are laying their plans to "buy" the council. It was however maintained that the scandal of the gas lease could not again be repeated now that the suspicions of the Philadelphian citizens had been awakened. The press, which remained absolutely silent throughout the six-weeks' subterranean working during which the gas company had hurried the lease through the council, dare not ignore a similar attack on the water department—at least so said the ex-mayor of Philadelphia—one of the opponents to the gas lease—who dined with us at Talcott Williams' in the evening.

Among other persons we met was the chairman of the Philadelphian board of education—a distinctly superior person of good social position. He and his colleagues were appointed by the judges: the board is absolutely controlled as to the extent of its expenditure by the city council—hence the large number of children who do not attend school, there being insufficient school accommodation and practically no compulsion on the children to go to school. The actual supervision of the schools and appointment of teachers (the applicants must have passed a qualifying examination) is in the hands of local *elected* boards. These boards are said, by the superior persons who constitute the central authority, to be purely mischievous. They are made up of inferior ward politicians "on promotion" to the city council; no attempt to abolish them has succeeded as the machine at Harrisburg (state legislature) is too powerful to allow the lowest rung of the political ladder to be wantonly cut away.

Usual sight seeing of university and usual address to students. Two nights at Bryn Mawr, luxurious women's college, day at Princeton (New Jersey) in charmingly situated university—Long talk with Professor Woodrow Wilson about recent developments in "congressional government." Attractive-minded man—somewhat like a young John Morley—literary in language, but with a peculiarly un-American insight into the actual working of institutions as distinguished from their nominal constitution. Stated that the complete subordination of the House to the Committee, and of the Committee to the Chairman, and of the Chairman to the Speaker and his two assistants (Committee of Rules) was comparatively new. He said that he asked Reed "where he was going to?" Reed said he did not know: that he just did what seemed to him most convenient at the moment. Wilson declared that Reed's rollicking sense of humour often led him to let the House misbehave itself so long as it did not interfere with his plans. Wilson deplores the recent charters of American cities. "The old illusion of the American people was faith in mass meetings, in the capacity of the mass meeting to conduct the work of government. To-day they rush to the other extreme and stake all on One Man." He believes that in the end they will accept representative institutions. I doubt it! [2]

❲*April 27th. New York*
After a morning spent in mending clothes and writing letters or in my diary, we determined to present our introduction (from Michael Davitt) to the Mayor of New York [Robert A. Van Wyck]. We did so with trepidation. New York "good society" had told us that Van Wyck was a low brute who had insulted the commander of a Spanish Vessel, snubbed the Commissioners of Education and generally displayed coarse manners. For some time we wandered through the municipal buildings trying to locate him. Groups of low looking men, some in dirt-begrimed clothes, others in flashy garments, were loitering in the passages and on the stairs.

2. Mrs. Webb wrote further about Wilson in a letter to one of her sisters. She identified him as the author of *Congressional Government,* a subject that "Bryce knew so much more of. . . ." "W. Wilson is much the most intellectual man we have met—has none of the *literalness* of most Americans—resembles a young and alert John Morley in appearance and temperament" (Beatrice Webb to Kate Courtney, New York City, April 29, 1898, in Passfield papers, British Library of Political and Economic Science, London School of Economics. All letters cited in this volume are from the Passfield papers).

Here and there a Tammany policeman laughed and chaffed with the rest. After much enquiry for the Mayor's Department we passed through a crowded little office full of loafers into the Mayor's reception room. Seated at a desk a bullet-headed little man with bristling moustache, ugly and unrefined, but with no mark of drink or other dissipation, and with a certain authority in his bearing, due, I imagine, to his career as a Police Magistrate. He was talking to a visitor in under-tones whilst the burly well-dressed doorkeeper stood by waiting to present our card and letter of introduction. We seated ourselves with others likewise waiting on the Mayor's pleasure. His private secretary—a common person of the ward politician type, was interviewing other visitors. The fat doorkeeper cracked jokes with other parties as they sauntered up to him to enquire whether the Mayor could see them. Presently the Mayor's visitor was dismissed and we were beckoned to the table; Mayor Van Wyck asked us to be seated, and after he had looked at the letter welcomed us with affability. "No introduction was needed Mr. Webb; now what can I do for you?" "Yes, I will send you straight up to the Council Chamber and then we will have a chat." So off we went with the doorkeeper—an uncouth rough customer with no education and no manners—to the two Chambers of Aldermen and Councillors. The same assemblage of common-looking individuals lounging in their comfortably padded chairs, smoking and reading whilst the clerk read through Bills and Ordinances. The Aldermen were sitting as Committee of the whole in private, but we gazed at them through a glass door—some sitting, others standing, most smoking—all looking equally unconcerned. As we re-entered the Mayor's room, Van Wyck appeared from a retiring room (he had apparently brushed himself up in the interval—for he looked more spruce and better groomed) and greeted us with great cordiality. He gave us a perfectly clear account of the procedure with regard to estimates and appropriations. Estimates were prepared in detail by the officials of the

Departments submitted in printed form to the Board of Estimates, boiled down by them into a Budget and then submitted to the Council. No increased expenditure could be made by the Council, only a reduction; and that could not be carried against the Mayor's veto except by ⅚th majority of both branches. The Mayor selected all officials and the Boards which were the administrative authorities were made up of officials. He was therefore supreme, as far as the Constitution was concerned, except that he could not remove an official after he had retained him for six months, without showing cause. "I made a clean sweep the day I came in, every official I could remove left on that day and *my* man took his place" (which means I suppose that Tammany had already parcelled out the places and that he was simply the agent of the organisation). All his answers to our questions were sensible and commonplace. He was against new expenditure, he was against interference, he was against the Albany legislature passing laws about New York City; "out of 250 Bills that came to me after the Albany Legislature had passed them I vetoed all except 12: My veto is absolute (in answer to a question from me) when the Legislature is not sitting. Governor [Frank S.] Black could not sign a Bill which I vetoed unless it was again passed by the State Legislature. As the Legislature will not probably sit for two years I have hung them up for a considerable time. Yes, we are perpetually fighting the State Legislature, protecting ourselves against their interference with our affairs. Delighted to see you any time Mr. Webb: I will introduce you to my secretary. Now Mr. Downs" he continued as the fat young man came forward, "this is Mr. Webb, a member of the London City Council; he comes here with an introduction from Mr. Davitt. Let him have anything he wants and see everything he wants to see; take him round to all the Departments and tell them that they are to put everything at his disposal. Good afternoon Mr. Webb: good afternoon Mrs. Webb: come and see me any time you like" and he sat himself down to sign documents brought by a clerk prior to interviewing a group of men who were seated in the background.

Dined in the evening at the Godkins [Edwin Lawrence Godkin] (Editor of the "Nation" and the "Evening Post") and met a party of the elite of the Reform and Philanthropic Section of "Good Society" in New York. They were vastly amused that we had seen their mayor and were going to see their City officials—would have been shocked if we had not been foreigners. Colonel Waring [George E. Waring, Jr.] (Head of the Street Cleaning Department under the Reform Administration of Mayor Stroz [William L. Strong]) was far more sensible and said that many of the Tammany officials were able and even upright men. Moreover, the power of removal had been checked by the State Civil Service law and only a small percentage of the municipal servants could actively be removed; practically only the Heads of Departments, and in some departments the lowest range of officials. Intermediate classes of clerks and the seconds in command were now irremovable except "on cause shown." Tammany did occasionally try to reduce their salaries and worry them into resigning, but public opinion was beginning to tell. He asserted that the Board of Estimates which had existed since the 1834 (?) Charter and which had complete control over the expenditure, had effectually checked malversation. "You may take it for granted that there is no theft from City funds now: Tammany makes its money indirectly in subscriptions from Corporations, and tips to speculators. What it does do, is to starve the departments in order to lower the tax rate and give away city franchises in order to fill the exchequer of Tammany Hall."

To-day we were in the Mayor's office soon after 10 o'clock by appointment with his secretary. Mayor Van Wyck was sitting at the table busily engaged signing documents and interviewing officials and other persons on city business (our impression is that American Mayors have a pretty hard life of it). The fat secretary had letters prepared for us and volunteered to take us straight up to the Comptroller's office. Here we saw the clerk to the Board of Estimates, a permanent official—a shrewd energetic little man with an apparent love of his work. He again explained the composition of the Board of Estimates (Mayor and two Heads of Departments appointed by him and two officials elected by the whole New York Constituency) and its way of transacting business. Objected hotly to the interference of the State legislature. "They force us to spend money on this or on that, and give us power to raise loans; but as we have reached our limit we cannot finish the works we have begun by their orders." (This limit to raising loans is constantly checking the efficiency of American cities) Believed in two chambers, because one checked the other. Objected vehemently to the incorporation of the Greater New York. Brooklyn had been running up its debt, all the local accounts were in confusion and the Board spent days and nights in getting matters straight. The electors voted for it because the question "Are you in favour of the New Charter" appeared on the straight list of every ticket, and as voters had been drilled into voting each ticket solid they unknowingly registered their vote for the Charter!

Afterwards visited City Clerks office and saw the second in command—the clerk to the lower chamber (Alderman). He was a permanent official—a lawyer by training, a shrewd sensible person who had made a considerable collection of books bearing on New York City. We noticed the same animus against the State Legislature for its "encroachment on original powers of the New York City of Colonial times. The power of the Municipal Assembly, he admitted, under the new Charter had been increased as compared to those of the Court of Aldermen (the single chamber of the last charter). But we could not make out that their powers of initiating or checking expenditure amounted to anything substantial. Their one financial power left undisturbed seems to be the granting of franchises, and under the New York

Charter they can only dispose of a franchise for 25 years. For some unexplained reason, the granting of a franchise is considered to be "Legislation"; the appropriation of a definite quota of the ratepayers' money to schools is deemed to be "administration."

Lunched with Dr. [Elgin R. L.] Gould, a young American statistician who has been made President or Managing Director of a new company of Philanthropic capitalists for the building of artisans dwellings and the sale of them to the occupiers. An individualist of the seventies, he struck us as a good fellow, irritatingly literal, and a bore. He entertained us to a sumptuous repast in the luxurious up-town City Club —the home of the "Good Government" party: a queer contrast to the shabby rough and tumble Tammany official in the ramshackle City Hall—with his shrewdness, public house affability and experience of men and things. There is a solid foundation of general capacity and human fellowship in Tammany, however corrupt its ways and bad its traditions. Tammany officials understand and sympathise with the niggardliness of the ratepayer and the anarchic objection to interference characteristic of the American "average sensual man."

❡[*April 29th.*
Visited yesterday [E. Ellery] Anderson, lawyer of good position, closely connected with Tammany. Offices on 14th floor of finest block in the city, with magnificent view of New York Harbour. Member of a Law Firm: large open office for clerks, long corridor out of which opened pleasantly furnished rooms for various partners of the firm. Anderson is a well-dressed, good looking elderly man with straightforward agreeable manners, expressing himself in cultured language —a contrast to the city official with his dirty clothes and ugly twang. From the view of the Harbour and the Cuban war we drifted on to the distinction between the Democratic and Republican parties. The Democrat represented the faith in

the responsibility of the individual; each individual being
like a "little dynamo working automatically for the good of
the community." The Republican, on the other hand, represented a faith in centralised power, in the capacity of the
few who are in authority at the centre of the State or the
Municipality to regulate the many and manage the affairs.*
That distinction declared Mr. Anderson, was still vital.
"Every man with intelligence" he emphatically asserted "was
born a Democrat or a Republican." As for the present leaders
of the two parties, of course, they each and all played to the
unthinking gallery who were incapable of understanding
these intellectual distinctions and thought only of personal or
class interests. As for Tammany Hall it was simply a logical
fulfilment of the requirements of Democracy. "So long as
you have universal suffrage" dogmatically asserted Mr. Anderson, "you will have corruption and theft and lack of
principle. . . . Water could not be purer than its source.
. . . Representatives of the common people would not be
better than the people who elected them. . . . they would
be of the earth, earthy. . . . The Reform Movement" continued Mr. Anderson with the consciousness of being a man
of the world "is Utopian: it is based on an absurdity—on
imagining that you can get men to do public work without
ulterior motive, without using their positions for pecuniary
gain. No man enters any other profession except for the
chances of personal advancement and pecuniary gain, why
should he go into politics for any other reason?" triumphantly
asked our lawyer. When we modestly stated that we had men
in England who gave up their time to Public Administration
without pay or chance of making anything out of it, and instanced the composition of the L.C.C. and other local authorities, Anderson looked politely sceptical. "Of course I think
that men with a stake in the country might be interested
themselves in its government: we are beginning to discover

---

* Very much the same definition as is given in Daniel Greenleaf Thompson's
Policies in Democracy.

that it will not do to let matters get too bad. I myself have always tried, by joining the machine, to keep it decent. Many years ago I and three other men started a revolt in the Democratic party from the methods of Tammany and created a rival machine, the County Democracy—We swept the boards in 1884(?), brought in our own Mayor and Court of Aldermen. But in a few years our machine had become as bad if not worse than Tammany—it was ruled by a little corrupt clique and bossed by one man. So I left it, and ever since then I have subscribed to Tammany Hall as the official organisation of my own Party in the City of New York."

We asked him how it came about that the Democrats, representing individualism, had joined hands with the Populists, "Extremes meet: men begin by believing in personal Liberty, get impatient and go over the line into extreme compulsion." "Why were the great Trusts allied with the Republican Party?" we asked. "The principle underlying these great combinations of Capital—these huge monopolies —is exactly the same" astutely answered Mr. Anderson, "as the principle underlying State Socialism. In both cases it is a concentration of power in the hands of a few, involving a subordination of the individual to a centralised authority. The Trusts and Syndicates feel that they are protected from the free enterprise of other individuals by protective tariffs, by legal rights, by every kind of artificial barrier, making it difficult for others to threaten their supremacy. It is quite natural they should think they will find support in the Republican Party."

With regard to New York City Government, he believed in the control of the Board of Estimates and thought the Municipal Assembly might just as well be abolished. When I asked my stock question, why the Charter had left the granting of the Franchise to the Municipal Assembly, he turned up the New Charter and showed me that before any Franchise was sold the Board of Estimates had to report on the adequacy of the price and *could withhold its consent.*

(This was not pointed out to me by the officials, who perhaps did not know it). "The problem of Franchises seems to be almost insoluble," he volunteered; "we are told that they ought to be sold by Public Auction. But what's the good of an auction at which there is only one bidder? Who would dare to bid against the Incorporated Gas Company with its millions of capital and its perfect plant for the franchise of lighting a new street? Then they say we ought to work the service ourselves: that means another nest egg of political corruption. I don't see any way out of the difficulty that a practical man can accept. We are on the horns of a dilemma and I tell the Reform Party it will take a thousand years to get off: so long as the American nation continues this experiment of Universal suffrage and Democratic Government —which I imagine they will for many years to come." The principle of Civil Service Examination he stated had been carried too far. It had been held by the State Civil Service Commission that an Inspector of Education must pass an examination. "Too absurd; if a business Corporation wants a lawyer, an engineer, or a surgeon, he is selected according to his past record; you don't subject him to an examination fit for a clever school boy. This stretching of the idea of examination to appointments of men of a certain age and standing is pure fanaticism, and like all fanaticism, it is unbusinesslike. Examination is all right for intermediate classes—but it is as unfit for the higher posts in which character and responsibility and experience are needed as it is for the general labourer where physical strength and regularity are the main requirements." To all of which we agreed. The Americans, with their love of logic and their odd lack of political common sense, are driving the examination idea too far. From our cynical lawyer we wandered round about Broadway trying to discover the location of various departments of the City Government. In bran new offices—bare of furniture and with boxes lying about packed with the papers and books of the former administration, we found the President of the

Board of Public Works and the newly elected statistical officer. The President was a jovial politician, ready enough to tell us everything about his Department. The Board consists as usual of Heads of Departments and the Mayor—five in all, two of these and the Mayor have been elected and two belong to the Mayor's Cabinet. Great works in process of construction, but all stopped because the Comptroller declared that the debt limit had been exceeded and no more bonds could be issued. All the labour directly employed by the Board was paid two dollars a day; and Mayor Van Wyck had publicly stated that in future all labour employed by contractors should be paid the same rate. They now do all the work by contract—even repairing sewers. The New Charter had thrown the whole City administration into confusion—"but we shall come straight in time," cheerily announced the President. The statistical officer we found alone in his empty office without clerks and in a state of abject helplessness. He had a turn for statistics and had the best of intentions but was hopelessly at sea. He was collecting, in a casual sort of way, the statistical reports of foreign municipalities, but had evidently given up as a bad job the statistics of his own city. "No statistics existed" he plaintively stated, and what did exist was now of little value since the New Charter had thrown everything into confusion. Altogether we came away with the impression that the Government of the Greater New York was at present in an Almighty Mess.

In the afternoon Colonel Waring, Reform Commissioner of Street Cleansing, came and called on us. He seems a thoroughly competent administrator, but a bad politician. From all accounts the administration of street cleaning gave universal satisfaction. Among other things he organised the street cleaners into a Trade Union and forced them to refer all their complaints through their representatives to a joint board of these and his officials. He said he was working for the de-consolidation of New York: it was a huge mistake and must be undone.

Tammany appears to be an easily understood organisation. The town is mapped out into Districts, each of which has its Boss serving on the Executive Committee. Under the District leader there are Captains, under these again a lower range of worker whose business it is to know a section of a street and report as to each man's circumstances and opinions. From the central office there is a constant flow of charity and kindness down to the humblest member of Tammany. Men who refuse to subscribe are intimidated, blackmailed and "spited" in every possible way in order to secure what Tammany calls "discipline." All salaries are assessed, and one of the few salaried officers of Tammany collects these dues as a matter of course. Thus human bonds are created throughout the community, of fellowship and helpfulness or of hate and "discipline" according to what happens to be a man's political opinions. When an opponent is strong enough he is respected, not molested. The Tammany Municipal policy is as I have already noted, economy and non-interference with private enterprise.

Dined with Joseph Choate—a leading New York lawyer; very similar to a distinguished London Q.C.; attractive, refined and cynical; an agnostic in politics, enjoying good dinners and smart society. He told brilliant stories exactly like Bowen used to, and he was especially swift and subtle in repartee. Utterly useless for our purpose, except that he promised to get us documents of the state convention over which he presided. We met there the same set as at Godkins —Good Society reformers. There is a graciousness and kindliness in American Good Society which is absent in the analogous set in London.

Lunched with Professor [E. R. A.] Seligman, wealthy Jew who lectures on Political and Economic Science at Columbia. Met Mayo Smith [Richmond Mayo-Smith], J. R. Clark [John Bates Clark] and others connected with Columbia. Same impression of second-rateness. Mayo Smith is a well-read man, seems to know all the English, German, American Economics

—but dull and literal, and with the personality of a superior elementary school teacher, or, as I said before, of a professor at a Realschule.

❨[*Monday 3rd.*

Mr. [James B.] Reynolds, Principal of the Settlement breakfasted with us. Excellent little man with progressive ideas and persistent kindly disposition. Agrees that it is impossible to run election campaigns on good government, and criticises society reformers for their anti-labour instincts; but asserts that good government party has a real issue in question of a permanent civil service. Tells many tales of Tammany; how the district leader is not only the centre of charity but the labour bureau of the district. The Surface Railway companies, when they have works on, or even for their regular service, give out to the district leader tickets entitling men to employment. Great corporations like the New York Central, will distribute free passes to the district leaders, to be given to desirable persons. Altogether Tammany plus the corporations are an elaborate network of corruption. The extravagance of the reform administration (necessitated, Reynolds asserts, by the rotten state in which every department was left—all buildings being in disrepair) offended the small house owner or shopkeeper. Described demoralisation of trade unions owing to political ambition of their leaders who were always selling themselves.

Interviewed Senator Canter [Jacob Aaron Cantor], leader of Democratic minority in the State Senate. Thick-set Jewish looking man, with black military moustache and the genial manners of a Ward politician. Member of a Law Firm (Jewish partners), represents Tammany at Albany. The organisation of parties in the Senate and the House much the same as in the Federal House of Representatives. The Speaker chooses Committees; majority members of Committees meet alone and announce their decisions to minority.

They seldom debate together. He told us little that was new about the machine. Explained that Corporations subscribed to both machines, but that Republicans had, as a national party, taken the Corporations under their wing. The feeling against the corporations was increased by the number of persons whom they could discharge in hard times; by reductions of wages and by their generally tyrannical conduct to employees. The Democratic party upheld the rights of the individual against the corporation and were always in favour of regulation of the conditions of employment. It had been captured by the Populists: a party organised by men who had not received office under Cleveland: the rank and file representing the socialistic element in the country. Cleveland had given great offence to his party by disregarding party lines in his appointments. And with this purity of administration he had favoured Wall Street and had been too intimately connected with the eastern money power. He gave us a graphic account of the Chicago convention at which [William Jennings] Bryan was chosen. When he (Canter) and other sound money Democrats got to Chicago they found the convention completely captured by Populists from south and west who gave the eastern Democrats to understand that they could join or break away as they liked, but that they should have no say. The whole convention was in a ferment. [Richard P.] Bland, an elderly silver propagandist being the probable candidate for President. But Bland could not speak and was either away or in the background. Then Bryan stepped forward and in magnificent voice penetrating to every quarter of the great hall delivered his oration. The whole convention was carried away with enthusiasm. "That speech makes him our candidate" I said to my fellow delegate from New York. "That speech could make a revolution" he answered, and we forthwith retired from the convention.

Senator Canter struck us as a "practical" party man, resenting the autocratic handling of the Democratic party by

Croker and welcoming the New Primary law as a possible
way out of it, but not inclined to do battle in favour of Good
Government.

Sidney lectured to students at Columbia in the afternoon.

❨[*May 4th.*

Tramped out with Miss [Lillian D.] Wald, Head-worker
of Nurses' Settlement, through the slums of New York—inhabited by Italians, Jews or Irish (no native Americans).
Tenement houses looking decent in front are horribly unsani-
tary. No air, no light, and bad accommodations. Struck me as
more unhealthy than our streets of little houses inhabited by
like people in London; rents higher than in London—8/- a
week for one room with little cupboards for the beds: 14/-
for respectable set where decent artisan family could live.
Unskilled women's wages evidently about the same as in
London. Italians are ousting Jews from lower branches of
factory trade: live cheaper and crowd more into a room.
Miss Wald states that the Jews are the best material for
citizenship of all the immigrants; least open to corruption
and anxious to be the good element. City Life. Large num-
bers voted for reform ticket last election. Irish worst because drunken and corrupt: Italians mere children—always
getting into trouble at police courts and much oppressed and
seared by the American methods—always looking forward to
returning to Italy with their earnings. Miss Wald states
that Miss Jane Addams's description of the Boss-system of
Chicago is photographic of her own experience of Tammany.

Another visit to the Mayor's secretary. The Mayor's office
with its crowd of chronic loungers, is much more like an ill-
conducted English Election Committee room than an official Department. The secretary was most good-natured. He
took us to the Floor of the Chamber of the popular and larger
branch of the Council. The President was a fool: order was
maintained by our friend Blake, the permanent clerk of the
Aldermen. Inconceivably low looking set of men: (some

Jews, more Irish) *—one face more repulsive than another in its cynicism, sensuality or greed. Here again I noted a peculiar type that one sees in all American representative assemblies: heavy jaw, aquiline nose, eyes bulging, sandy hair, the main features of the face being embedded in unhealthy looking fat. The type combined the characteristics of a loose liver, a stump orator and intriguer with the vacant stare of the habitual lounger. Other members difficult to describe in their indefiniteness, but all seemed endowed with highly developed jaws and undeveloped heads. Business conducted in usual infantile fashion. No agenda: only a calendar containing resolutions and old business. Reports of Committees of Administrative Boards, read out mechanically by an illiterate clerk. Meanwhile the assembly chattered; occasionally it was called upon to vote in a haphazard sort of way, on a resolution appended to a Report heard and understood by a mere fraction of those present. Now and again there would be dissent and a formal vote taken by calling each member's name. In the middle of the voting a member would jump up, and under the plea of asking to be excused from voting would begin to debate the question, volunteering new information or disputing the procedure of the committee, or bringing in another issue. When he had said his say he would withdraw his plea to be excused from voting and proceed to cast his vote for or against! Indeed, the only debates with any vitality in them took place *during the process of voting.* Any individual member could transfer his veto—after the vote had been taken or could propose that the House "reconsider the question." Note too that any ordinance affecting particular persons (for instance, trading licenses) was always referred to the Alderman of the district in which the person concerned resided for his Report—a nice little dodge to enable the Alderman to *"give* away" something.

From the Aldermen's chamber we went to the Council.

* Judge Power states that the government of the City under Tammany is almost exclusively in the hands of Irishmen and Jews.

Exactly the same type of member and the same procedure. The clerk was drawling out an elaborate ordinance or Bill, drafted by the Committee on Law, settling the terms on which licences for pedlars should be granted. This question really seemed to interest the assembly and various amendments altering terms in a chaotic way, were inserted into the already badly drafted Bill. The Chairman of the Committee mildly protested that the representatives of "a Pedlar's district" were so lowering the fine for not taking out a licence that it would encourage evasion, it being cheaper to pay numerous low fines than to pay for the licence. "The gentleman comes from a well-to-do district: but I'm the man that paid 46 fines in one day for my constituents; one dollar fine is high enough. And I don't see why the gentleman should object: it won't injure him and it will be a blessing to the poor folk," was the pertinent plaint of a bleared-eyed corpulent people's legislator. Of course, the popular motion was carried. A discussion then arose as to whether the Clerk was reading the text correctly and whether the text submitted by the Committee was typographically corrected. When the business was disposed of, the next business was the reading of the report of the Highways Committee ending in a resolution in favour of an extension of a particular street. By the time the vote was half taken, a member jumped up and stated that the Committee had never met and therefore could not report. In the anarchic procedure that followed— the original resolution passed, re-consideration passed, explanations during the vote by all the members of the committee—we completely lost count of what was happening as I think did the majority of the members. At last the assembly got impatient and voted something final by a large majority, but I failed to discover what the vote meant. Returned to Mayor's office to the meeting of the Board of Estimates ("Executive Session"—therefore not public) just over. A cordial good-bye to good-natured fat Secretary and we saw the last of New York City Government.

Beatrice Webb

Beatrice and Sidney Webb

Dined in the evening with Judge [Francis M.] Scott, Judge
of Supreme Court of New York State. "The greatest black-
guard in New York" we were told by some of the Reformers.
From being a "Reform candidate" for Mayor many years
ago, he became Corporation counsel under Mayor Strong.
Last autumn he finally "came to terms" with Tammany and
secured the Tammany nomination for the Supreme Court.
A tall, thick-set man, with heavy jaw and disagreeable coarse
features, he looks more the Ward politician than the professional lawyer. Of strong will and good brains, his expression
is discontented and soured, as if he had sold himself and
not got his price. Frank and cynical in conversation: "Human nature is everywhere the same: you can only appeal
to its self-interest or to its vanity." His description of the
Tammany machine was detached. In old days each powerful Corporation had its paid representative at Albany, either
in the Legislature itself or as a Lobbyist. Now the system
has completely changed. He knew a lawyer who had done
all the business of the Erie Board. He met him a little while
ago and asked him why he was never at Albany. "Oh," said
his friend, "it's not necessary to go to Albany: I just go over
the way to Platt or Croker and arrange matters with them.
Far more satisfactory to both parties." Scott agreed that the
present subsidies from Corporations to the Machines were
chiefly to protect themselves against black-mail, not to buy
concessions. "They have got all the legislation they want:
now they want to be protected against blackmail measures
imposing restrictions or the creation of the franchises for rival
corporation;" cynically added the Judge. Disapproved of
New Charter: drawn up by men who had no technical knowledge: ill thought out amalgam of the separate charters of
the constituent cities of Greater New York.

Mrs. Scott, the leader of the Anti-Suffrage Movement, a
talkative, clever, shrewish wife, hard and brittle in tone,
entertaining me after dinner with her lively account of the
way she check-mated the Suffrage women at Albany. By the

time the men came up from dinner she and I were discussing the relative position of English and American women, and I was drawing "a long bow" concerning the confidential relations between English husband and wife: how the English wife was always consulted in business and political emergencies. "You don't mean to tell me that the English politician introduces his political associates to his wife or consults her as to his political alliances?" asked Judge Scott in the deep tones of honest horror.

([May 5th. En route for Cornell.

Lunched yesterday with Judge Powers—Commissioner of Aqueducts in New York City. An Irish adventurer and genial ruffian, handsome in feature and easy and terse in language, with a good heart, wide experience of men, personal courage and independence, he has always been a "kicker" against Tammany and has never belonged to Tammany Hall. In a better social environment he might even have become honest and public spirited. Judge Powers, in fact, sympathetic, witty and strong, was the first attractive "practical" politician we have met. As he leisurely filled himself with food he gave us, in elaborate phrases and with genial winking, an elaborate account of the evolution of New York City Government and the organisation of Tammany. His account was racy and I wished I could transcribe it verbatim. (Travelling in a Pullman car with closed windows and hot air is not conducive to graphic writing.)

The Mayor, Aldermen and Council of New York City began as a fully developed autonomous municipality. But during the Civil War, Home Rule was virtually withdrawn, the State legislature passing all ordinances, authorising expenditure, levying tax rates and practically carrying on the City government. When the time came to re-endow the City with its powers the Tweed Ring was in office (1890?), and fearful of downfall, managed to get through the State Legislature a Charter which vested the real authority in a Board of Estimates which could not be removed from office for six years. "So by a fluke," declared Judge Powers, "We were given the one municipal institution in which the "ordinary citizen now believes. Since that time our City Government has become steadily less democratic. Now that the granting of Franchises has been placed under the virtual control of the Board of Estimates the Municipal Assembly might just as well not exist."

Tammany exists, the Judge declared, because there exist in an American city individuals "who live by the sword." They are men with no training, with no technical knowledge and therefore incapable of earning their livelihood by a profession or a trade. On the other hand they are men with social gifts, with an instructive appreciation of the lower kind of human motive, with a capacity for discerning what individuals and classes most desire. They are nearly always "good fellows," ready to sit up half the night in a club room or spend half a day doing some little kindness—obtaining employment for this man, acting as bail for another, getting "free" legal advice for husband in trouble and charitable assistance for the wife. To this species belong the working members of Tammany Hall. They aim at popularity each in his own neighbourhood; they are friends with the saloon keepers and with other caterers to public needs, more especially of disreputable needs; their first step is to join the Ward Democratic club, they make themselves assiduously useful to the District Boss: they presently find themselves picked out to be Captains of electoral districts. Thus a District Boss will be surrounded by a bodyguard of men whom he has made and who are likely to be loyal to him; whilst he himself has been selected in much the same fashion by Croker from his personal following and owes everything to him. It is these innumerable chains of personal obligation binding man to man; the common run of inhabitants with the Captain of the Electoral District, the Captains with the District Boss; the District leaders with Croker that constitute the framework of Tammany Hall. This organisation is inspired by the personal loyalty of the Irish to their leaders and maintained by the spoils system in the municipal services and wholesale favoritism in administration whereby all claims are eventually liquidated. If a District leader revolts and tries to stand "on his own," he fails to get office, his captains are ignored, his constituency unprotected, and his district deliberately starved in all its services. Presently he finds it better either to knuckle under or to leave the business, and his Captains carefully elect, as District leader, a man who is in favor with the Head Boss—from whom all favors flow.

([En route for [   ]
Cornell University May 7th
Stayed two nights with Professor [Jeremiah W.] Jenks—lecturer of Political Science. From his appearance, manner and speech I should have taken him for a pushing and enterprising manager of store in a Western city. His wife and children are what we should call in England ultra lower-middle class, talking with a detestable twang and dropping "h's."; they are kindly and good-natured, but they have neither tact nor grace nor charm of any kind: their clothes are ugly and not over clean. The one redeeming feature is the house. Alike in construction and furniture it is simple, pretty and convenient, without tawdriness or crude colouring. The native woods of the sliding doors, of the parquet floors, of the mantlepieces and chairs, combine variety in tone, dignity of form with restfulness and harmony. Certainly Americans understand domestic architecture. Good taste in interiors is the rule and not exceptional as in England. Professor Jenks himself is a strong self-controlled and sensible fellow, pre-eminently sane in his views on all things; alert to observe for himself, at any rate all superficial matters, and anxious to get at the actual living fact and not rest content like so many University Professors with mere book

knowledge. But he has a purely business brain and seems
singularly out of place as a Professor. One wonders whether
he would not have done better to have remained in the store
in which he was apprenticed or to have become a corn dealer
or timber merchant like his two brothers. Certainly his dominant purpose seems to be to increase his income by small
economies and extra efforts. It is perhaps difficult with English prejudices to be fair to such a man in such a position.
The ugliness of the family group is so obtrusive that their
association with University life seems grotesque and almost
revolting. So too the president of the university (Shurman
[Jacob Gould Schurman]) a peculiarly repulsive type; pushing and unsensitive, with the unctuousness of the popular
nonconformist preacher and family grocer combined! And
yet one feels latent in the man the domineering disposition
of the business boss. Intellectually he is an eclectic in the
shallowest sense; always eager to open new departments,
with a preference for the more mechanical and flashy kind of
knowledge. But in spite of this unfavourable introduction to
Cornell, there is a good deal of interest and hopefulness in
the institution. It was founded by a self-made man—intent
on establishing a university for the "working-men," at which
youths might get university education whilst they were earning their livelihood. The complete realisation of this was, of
course, impossible in a day university in a remote corner of
the state. The majority of students are drawn from the propertied middle-class who can afford to keep their sons at
college. But quite a number of the students do actually support themselves by waiting at table at the fraternities (self-
governing boarding houses of the richer young men), by
doing odd jobs in the little town and in the university. And
this menial occupation does not mark these students out,
owing to the real spirit of social equality at Cornell. Besides
this refreshing absence of snobbishness there is a spirit of
freedom and adventure in the academic life of Cornell: the
students electing what they will study. Every year sees new

developments and experiments in the curriculum. And I imagine from Morse Stephen's account that among the 200 professors there are quite a few men of real distinction and good breeding though in common with Morse Stephens they cordially hate the president and rather avoid association with the Jenks type of colleague.

Morse Stephens (author of a History of the French Revolution) a brilliant and accomplished man who was for one reason or another a failure in England, has settled down at Cornell as lecturer on modern history. He is an eccentric: a scholar more than a gentleman. His dirty untidy bachelor ways; self-indulgence in eating, expansive and paradoxical intellect, racy, indiscreet and exaggerated speech, not to mention his restless vanity—all these qualities or defects—make him offensive to many good people. But with his broad and highly cultivated mind, paradoxical wit, and vigorous language, we found him a blessed relief from the commercial faculties and literal phrases of the ordinary American professor of the Jenks type. Morse Stephens was avid of news of his English friends, so we smoked and chatted all the afternoon in Jenks' little library—perhaps not a very well-bred performance, since the Jenks family were necessarily out of it! So Mrs. Jenks may now be remarking on the insolence of English manners. However, I made up for it by captivating the affections of the little Jenks—their proud mother informing me at breakfast that they had voted me "a real peach!"

Morse Stephens is, on the whole, delighted with his American life. "I am petted, Mrs. Webb, I am taken for a genius, I am allowed to talk; I am even handsomely paid for it. And the country is intensely interesting—so vast—there is room for everybody here, and everyone is appreciated. When I remember the deadly convention of Oxford and Cambridge —the chilliness of English life, the refusal to accept talent unless it takes certain defined and traditional forms, I feel inclined" (looking round and perceiving the Jenks were, for the moment, out of the room) "to feel charitably towards that loathsome president of ours who is always on the look out for a new science or a new man." "Loathly person!" said the English professor in a tone of disgust, "I refuse to have anything to do with him. He would dismiss me if he dared; but my classes are too successful."

"American boys, dear creatures" replied Morse Stephens to a question from me, "thoroughly well-mannered; never seen any brutality or grossness among them—the nearest approach to viciousness is their detestable habit of chewing gum. But they have not the same sense of honour as English boys; they make excuses; you can't trust them; they are always adapting themselves to you, instead of letting you get some real influence over them. All comes from being brought up by women; living at home with their mothers and sisters; being taught by women teachers, and sitting next little girls at school. It improves their morals and manners and lowers their sense of honour and public spirit."

"Never been inside the house before" remarked Morse Stephens as we sauntered out into the Campus. "Professors at an American University are a queer medley. There are some men who would be first rate in any European university; there are others who ought to be still on the farm or behind the counter from whence they came—Look at our President —*loathly creature*" repeated Morse Stephens, his corpulent form heaving with repugnance. "But I have never been so happy since my undergraduate days," he continued in grateful tones. "Look at this view" waving his fat hand towards the beautiful blue lake, at the base of the wooded hill upon which the University stands—"look at that expanse of water and wooded hill stretching for miles into an almost unknown country—the feeling that there is a whole continent before you; if one place does not suit you, another will. And the life is so interesting" reiterated Morse Stephens "always fresh developments. These dear people, always starting their new experiments in such deadly earnest; taking themselves so seriously; really believing that they are getting better and better, wiser and wiser—certain that they are getting richer and richer—every year, every month, every day. And the further west you go the stronger the feeling of restless hopefulness—no distinctions, no sense of proportion—only an undiscriminating pushing forwards towards new persons, new methods, new things. Oh! it is fine, Mrs. Webb: it is fine."

In the evening some dozen working men came up to talk to Sidney—Morse Stephens unable to tear himself away from English friends sitting back in his chair smoking cigars and silently listening to our cross-examination of these working-class aldermen as to the troubles of a little city government. As usual the municipal council has been stripped of all its powers except voting appropriations and disposing of franchises. A special Board of Paving has been created: nominated by the Mayor—which resolutely refused to permit the Board of Aldermen to add as a rider to its appropriation for paving a recommendation as to which street should be paved, what wages paid, what hours worked by the contractors' men. They were simple folk, these working class representatives of working class wards—all Trade Unionists —a glass blower, a carpenter, a tram driver, and some other tradesmen. They were obviously at the mercy of the Mayor and the Executive Boards, nominated by the Mayor.

([Vassar University.

Travelled down to Syracuse with a company of Cornell students: well-mannered but somewhat unhealthy looking youths, bad teeth, spotty complexions, narrow chests and sloping shoulders. Perhaps a third of them were chewing gum. There was no approach to horse-play, no loud talk or vulgar chaff as there would have been in a company of English youths of the same class; and from their expressions and polite ways with women one can quite believe the accuracy

of Morse Stephen's statement. Even if they were alone together there would be no indecent jokes or foul words. This
atmosphere of personal purity, gentleness of manner and universal good-temper, is extremely agreeable in the U.S.A. One
never despairs of human nature as one is apt to do when
one watches the crude animalism and coarse insolence of
some of our English middle-class folk.

Another simple refined little home. Professor [Herbert Elmer] Mills (Political Economy Professor at Vassar) is a slip
of a man with pretty features and gentle ways—the son of a
New England Baptist Minister and a grandson of Rochdale
weavers. The wife is a plain old-maidish person, also from
New England, with natural refinement and tact. The house
and furniture simple and in good taste; the fare plain almost
to scantiness! * The Mills couple were a welcome relief
from the crass ugliness of the Jenks family; though I doubt
whether Mills is as able as Jenks, or whether Mrs. Mills
could translate an Italian MSS. as Mrs. Jenks announced she
was doing!

Professor Mills, with American helpfulness, had asked up
the present Mayor the first evening, and two past mayors
yesternight. Poughkeepsal City Government follows the exemplar of New York. The Board of Aldermen made up of
the "poor timber" (to use an American expression), of the
ward politician, has been stripped of its powers by Government charters. Four Special Commissions rule the little city
through administrative departments. Two of these commissioners are elected by the whole city and are therefore, it is
said, far better men than if they were elected by wards. The
Fire Department has, however, been left in the hands of the
Aldermen, with the result that two of them are now under
indictment for being bribed by a manufacturer of hose.

* Breakfast 8 o'clock begins with a cooked cereal and cream; then an egg
and coffee: dinner one o'clock, soup, roast meat, vegetables, and if there is
a party—ice cream, black coffee: "Lunch" about 7 o'clock: consisting of tea,
bread and butter and shrimps. Prices of food seem almost identical with
England: food costs 4 persons and little boy £2 a week.

◖[*May 16th. Harvard.*

Three days staying with Professor [William James] Ashley
and his wife at Harvard. Harvard society much like that of
Oxford or Cambridge. Leisurely culture in the dominant
note. President [Charles W.] Eliot is a courtly 18th century
sort of person; a rigid individualist in politics and religion;
combining like most New England aristocrats, personal dignity with simplicity of manners. The American tradition of
"choose equality" gives to the manners of the "old New England" families, a charm and perfect breeding unknown in
English Society. They are an aristocracy, but they are an
aristocracy that accepts all their fellow citizens as their
social equals.

"When he is not a practical * politician he is a visionary"
said the precise and correct young Charles [Francis] Adams—Mayor of Quincy ³ of "Jo" Quincy Mayor of Boston.†
Both belong to the blue blood of New England: both alike
are men of sufficient means to devote themselves, in the English sense, to politics. But Adams is universally accepted as
a charming irreproachable young man, a fit match for the

* "Practical" means corrupt in American political terminology.
† The following letter (dated December 11, 1897) from the well-known
philanthropist E. D. Mead gives the current estimate of Mayor Quincy in
"Reform" circles. "I must tell you of the great pleasure with which I have
read your letter in the Herald about Quincy and the blatheskite Republican
attacks upon him. It will accuse the City of Boston of softening of the brain
if such criticism avails. Quincy has done wrong, I think, in paying some
political debts in pretty small coin, when he has been forced into tight places.
But I believe he has always done it to placate men whom he was anxious to
coerce into service for good and large things. I believe immensely in his
fundamental purpose and in his ever purer and purer methods. No other
municipal administrator in this country has equal knowledge of the great
municipal movement in the modern world or is so impressed by its spirit. He
has great imagination and looks at Boston in a great way. The making of the
greatest mayor we ever had is in him. Men who do not see this, citizens of
Boston who do not act upon it, are to be pitied. I am glad that a Republican
like you sees the conflict in its true proportions, despises all this wind and
clap-trap as it deserves to be despised, and is not afraid to say so with
vehemence."

3. Charles Francis Adams was mayor of Quincy in 1896–97, but not in
1898. In 1898 he became treasurer of Harvard College, a position he held
until 1929. He married Frances Levering in April, 1899.

most fastidious Boston girl, whilst Jo Quincy, though admired for his administrative capacity, is frowned upon as being uncouth in manner, "too much of a Politician," too completely "in with" the machine. Moreover, though both are Democrats, Adams has sought salvation among the gold Democrats, (a party singularly like in type to the Liberal Unionists minus Chamberlain), whilst Quincy has publicly given in his adhesion to the Chicago platform. For the rest, Adams is a polite young man, commonplace in thought, ultra correct in expression, with the usual society chit chat and the pleasant gallant ways towards women which are but so many devices for showing the fair ones that they are essentially inferior to the male. Jo Quincy, on the other hand, is reported to dislike women, and though stiffly polite in his manner, he has never been known to pay a compliment or say a pretty word. Stiffness of bearing, sombreness of expression, an aloofness from all the little amenities and personalities of social life, a short jerky address, as if he felt constrained to speak to you and found no pleasure in it, an absence of humour or "sympathy" or desire to please, all these characteristics have made him thoroughly unpopular with the Back Bay set in Boston. To us he is distinctly attractive. He is, to begin with, remarkably good looking—tall and slight, well-shaped head and features, deepset brown eyes, sensitive intellectual expression—irreproachably dressed, quite the hero from the pages of a novel. In physical type he is like the Balfours—specially Gerald Balfour. He will talk "shop" for hours together: his mind concentrating itself alternatively on abstract theory and the practical possibilities of particular forms of municipal enterprise. It adds a certain romance to his personality that in spite of his aristocratic aloofness and stiffness, and a total absence of good fellowship, he is the Boss of the Democratic machine; and has complete mastery of its inner workings. In short he is the "Parnell" of Irish Boston, substituting for Home Rule, Fabian Collectivism as the goal towards which he is working. Accord-

ing to universal testimony Quincy has been singularly successful alike in increasing his personal power and in using it
to promote municipal enterprise in almost every direction.
"Good Society" accuses him of having won this success by
compromising with the mammon of unrighteousness—the
Spoils System—of having truckled, in his patronage, here
to the Catholics, there to the Trade Unionists; of having even
given a share of the party offices to Jews and Italians in order to "round off" his political influence. And it may be
added, he does not deny it. "How far do you consider it
necessary to consult the Ward Politician in your appointments?" I asked. (Quincy is a man it pays to be direct with)
"Well" he jerked out looking straight in front of him "in the
unpaid Boards not at all. In appointments to these unpaid
offices I consider exclusively personal fitness. With regard
to the highest-paid officials I give political exigencies a certain consideration. In the employment of labour—political
considerations dominate, providing always there is no question of actual incapacity. I should not appoint an absolutely
incapable man, who happened to be a political supporter.
But right political opinions would be an almost essential
qualification. The good word of the ward leader would give
a man a decided 'pull.' " The cross-examination has not been,
however, exclusively on our side. The many hours we have
spent together—a long drive in the Parks on Saturday, an
expedition down to Manchester-on-Sea on Sunday—have
been quite as much occupied by questions from him on London government, on the theory of municipal administration,
and the technical details of labour legislation, and on Trade
Union activities in England as by questions from us with
regard to his administrative work in Boston or his political
associations with the Democratic Party.

BOSTON MUNICIPAL GOVERNMENT

By the present charter the whole executive government of
Boston is vested in the Mayor. He appoints various Boards
(some paid and others unpaid) and certain officials at the

heads of Departments. These Boards are always on the increase: Quincy's policy being subdivision of Labour and the appointment of experts for each department. Very recently a Board of Apportionment has been created which will decide all estimates: the Municipal Council retaining only the right to reduce a particular vote, and this limited right is subject to the Mayor's veto. The Council (or Lower House) has practically no power, the little remnant of authority left to the representative assembly being concentrated in the Board of Aldermen or the Upper House. The Board of Aldermen can veto the Mayor's appointments; grant franchises and otherwise make itself objectionable by passing ordinances about street lamps and licences. In appearance the members are a better lot than in the New York or Philadelphian Common Councils. But by repute there is the same petty corruption, and blackmail "deals" between them and Corporations. The Mayor has hitherto been unable to get some of his most important appropriations passed because the members of both chambers insist on the city's income being doled out in improvements to the various electoral districts, partly to gain patronage and partly to have something to show at the forthcoming election. Thus the Mayor has been forced to go straight to the State Legislature for special acts, forcing the Municipal Assembly to sanction new loans and new expenditure. The State Legislature has been, in fact, a supreme Municipal Council ready to insist on any necessary expenditure which the Common Council refused. The Representative body is, therefore, in Boston as elsewhere, a fifth wheel in the coach, chocked up with corrupt transactions, thus preventing the administrative machinery from working smoothly. In order to get his appointments or appropriations passed the Mayor will make "deals" with the Board of Aldermen in respect to particular appointments. The good work of the Municipal administration begins and ends with the Mayor and his unpaid advisers. Quincy has shown consummate skill in enlisting, either as confidential advisers or as members of Executive Boards, the prominent citizens of Boston. All the distinguished Boston families we have come across contribute a member to these Boards, either the husband or the wife or the son. Thus whilst he has kept in with the political machine by scattering paid appointments and positions among the ward politicians he has placated "good society" by making it responsible for the policy of the municipality on special subjects. Thus Boston has, on the whole, a most enlightened Government somewhat indifferently carried out: Boston is administered by public spirited and well-informed brains, and corrupt and inefficient hands. The city of Boston is in fact governed by its aristocracy working through a corrupt democracy.

It is impossible for an outsider to estimate the net result. The Park Department, for instance, with its playgrounds and bathing places, its open spaces and gardens, seems almost ideal. The municipality has been far-sighted enough to "condemn," that is to resume ownership according to the legal doctrine of the Right of Eminent Domain, large tracts of shore, hill and dale, so that the public grounds of Boston extend for miles around whilst including bathing grounds in the very centre of the city. These gigantic operations have been rendered possible by the Massachusetts law (similar to that of New York) of enabling a Public Authority to take any land it chooses paying afterwards to the owners the market price of the land and buildings (but giving no compensation to trade interests).

On the other hand the members of the Education and Poor Law Boards complain bitterly of the inefficiency of their departments and tell graphic stories of political milkmen who "deliver" 40 quarts of milk too much every day to public institutions; or politically appointed compositors who charge eight times over the same "copy" and so on.

To complete this sketch it should be added that certain services are performed by State-appointed Boards having jurisdiction over the group of cities of which Boston is the principal: the Park system, the Water and the Sewage.

We have had a glimpse of a State Government. The Massachusetts' Legislature is a dignified body: the members being for the most part representative citizens. As the Republicans are in an overwhelming majority there is no party cleavage. The same inefficient procedure, and lack of leadership, but a far higher level of intelligence and integrity than in any other American Representative Assembly we have yet seen. Governor [Roger] Wolcott (to whom we were introduced) is a fascinating personage—old New England family—a splendidly handsome man, with tact and charm, integrity and a fair intelligence, married to an equally charming woman (one of the Presscotts [Prescotts]). Here again the State is ruled by its aristocracy. It is also represented in the U.S. Senate by Lodge and Hoare [George F. Hoar]—two wealthy and well-connected personages. We have had no opportunity of understanding the inside working of the State Government as the war preparations absorbed the Governor, and the Session of the Legislature was drawing to an end. There is, however, a sweet flavour about Massachusetts government—whether of its State or of its many municipalities that marks it out from the Federal Government in Washington and from the State and Municipal Government of Virginia, Pennsylvania and New York.

⟨

(*The following is a joint entry in S[idney] W[ebb]'s handwriting.*)

Interviewed Osborn [Osborne] Howes, Secretary of an Insurance Company, who had been the leading member of a small commission appointed by the State Legislature to consider the question of a "Greater Boston"—the consolidation of Boston with the 20 or 30 smaller cities and townships lying within 10 miles of it, and collectively equalling it in population. This alert and well-informed business man is one of the regular leader-writers for the Boston Herald, the best news-

paper. To him the device of "Metropolitan Boards" for Parks, Water and Drainage seemed only a temporary expedient. Such unrepresentative bodies, appointed by the Governor, and spending large sums as they pleased, to be charged on the cities, could not possibly endure. The Parks Board, for instance, though universally approved, had been unable as yet to collect one penny of its expenses. When its large outlay began to be "apportioned" (this is done by a separate commission appointed ad hoc by the Supreme Court of the State) according to the local benefits, so much objection was made that the Legislature put the whole thing off by allowing all maintenance expenditure up to 1900 to be charged to capital; and "loaning the State credit" to enable the Park Board to borrow all it needed up to that date. Thus the magnificent Parks and Reservations of the suburban belt of Boston—the Blue Hill mountains and so on—though begun five years ago have as yet not cost one cent to the taxpayers! No wonder the Board is popular, and no objection is made to its undemocratic proceedings.

Osborne Howes and his colleagues reported against simple annexation to Boston of all the outlying townships and cities —partly because they found this generally unpopular. Though the outside cities have usually a higher tax rate than Boston, and might gain pecuniarily by absorption, their citizens resented the idea of being swamped by the reputed "corruption" and machine politics of the larger city, and also feared that they would lose all local life.

He favoured the establishment of some form of "County Government," the creation of a County Board for certain Metropolitan District purposes, whilst leaving each city and township its existing independent government for local purposes. With this idea, he had visited England, and especially the London County Council late in 1895. Falling into the hands of the Moderates there, notably Lord Onslow, he had derived the impression that the L.C.C. was unpopular, that the Progressives would be hopelessly smashed at the next elec-

tion in 1898, and that the Conservative Government would
divide up London into 15 to 20 separate cities. This rather
discouraged him, and as the Commissioners were unable to
frame any satisfactory constitution for the proposed Metropolitan Council, they made an inconclusive report, as regards
any constructive policy, and it has not been acted upon.

Visited also Mr. John Woodbury, the salaried secretary of
the Parks Board. This Board, which is appointed by the Governor and is unpaid, has handsome offices high up in a tall
building in the centre of Boston, from the windows of which
it can survey the circle of hills which bounds the basin forming its field of operations. It is also connected by telephone
with all its outlying parks. The Secretary, an enthusiast for the
Board and its work. It arose in 1890 out of a movement in the
Appalachian Mountain Club—a local miniature "Alpine Club"
—with the idea of preserving mountain tops &c. largely instigated by [Charles] Eliot, now deceased, the gifted and charming son of President Eliot of Harvard. Through his efforts, the
legislature incorporated a voluntary board of Trustees empowered to receive gifts of places of natural beauty, to be held
for public use. This promptly got itself converted into a Commission to enquire into a Park System for Greater Boston. Eliot
wrote the report, an inspired document, painting such a pic-
ture of the possibilities of an extended Park System that influential public opinion was converted at once, and the report has
ever since remained the charter and guide of the Park Board.
The Board itself was created in 1893, and empowered to spend
a million dollars, raised by loan. Since then the legislature has
gone on annually enlarging its total operations by a million or
so dollars at a time, all charged to capital and raised by bonds.
The Board has as yet done practically nothing in the way of
laying out its purchases, contenting itself with gradually ac-
quiring a series of "Reservations," connected with strips of
meadow and avenues. Boston and some other of the larger
cities in the area maintain their own parks. The Blue Hill
Mountains and a "beach" seem the principal acquisitions.

Waiving the question of the constitution of the Board, and its peculiar finance, it seems to me to embody an admirable idea, and to represent something in advance of England. Every great city has an interest in preserving parks within a wide radius, and yet has usually no power to spend money on them. The outlying villages, on the other hand, destined to become suburban, neither can nor will realise their future destiny, and have no interest in large capital outlays to provide breathing spaces for the future expansion of the city.

There ought to be a public body charged with the preservation and acquisition of parks and woodlands within the radius of 50 miles round London; and a similar authority to deal with a suitable area round Liverpool and other large cities.

Boston here gives us a useful suggestion for use at home, though we can perhaps improve on the finance of Boston's Park Commission, and on its constitution. The first step is clearly to find an Eliot to write a report on the possibilities of a Home Counties Park Commission!

❨20 May/98. Last night I attended the meeting of the City Council, the lower branch of the Municipal Legislature.

(Professor D. R. [Davis Rich] Dewey took me—he is Professor of Economics at the Institute of Technology, where elementary economics is part of the compulsory course of its 1,200 students—for the most part young men of 16–20 studying engineering &c. Dewey lectures to a class of 250 or so, and has only one assistant. I remember him in the same place 10 years ago. He was then a youthful enthusiast, fresh from graduation, and full of hopes from what he called the "laboratory method" of teaching economics—setting the students to work out from blue books their own statistical tables, construct their own curves, and compile their own histories of particular trades from the published records. Now he is sobered and a little discouraged. These crowds of elementary students do not respond to such methods. He sees now that lecturing is as much as they will absorb. He is discontented with all the economic textbooks, and has just been writing round to all the economics professors to find out what they used—the answers are [Francis A.] Walker, [Richard T.] Ely, [Charles] Gide, [Arthur T.] Hadley—not much [John Stuart] Mill (as at Harvard) or [Alfred] Marshall. He is hankering after a descriptive economics, but says it must not be a child's book: it must be difficult reading enough to earn the respect of adult students.)

The Council was the lowest depth in representative bodies that we have yet explored. Its powers are limited practically to concurring with the Aldermen in voting the appropriations. It has no patronage, and was until lately not paid. The members then gave themselves carriage-rides and dinners, so now they get £60 a year ($300) in lieu. It is an assembly of 75 members, elected three each by 25 wards; 42 were Democrat and 33 Republican. The position is evidently despised, not only by the good citizen, but even by the Ward politician of any standing, for half the members were youths between 20 and 35, striplings describing themselves as law students, medical students, clerks, telegraphists, stenographers, with half a dozen bartenders and billiard markers. The President was a short, slight, stripling of 30. I saw only one man of 50 among the whole 75. There were two young negroes (law students) two Russian Jews (very sensible men, small dealers) and about thirty Irish—three different Donovans for instance. There were car-drivers, hackmen, labourers and mechanics; a few little grocers, a peddler or two—the whole forming the queerest debating society kind of legislative body I ever saw. But the council had a beauté de diable—these young men, with the cleanest of collars and cuffs, and nice jacket suits, had a distinctly more pleasing appearance than the flashy, overfed dissipated ward politicians of the New York and Philadelphia Councils. What they most resembled was the debating society of a London polytechnic Institute.

The same crude and imperfect procedure—forms identical with those of Congress, as also the arrangement of the chamber, the President on his raised dais and square table, with clerks below him, and all the paraphernalia of officials around him. (This body costs Boston in stipends alone, for members and officials, over £8,000 a year, and is worth less than nothing).

The procedure of the "motion to reconsider" seems to amount usually to this, that after every resolution passed, one of the members "moves to reconsider:" the President announces that "Mr. Jones moves reconsideration, hoping the same will not prevail!" It is then formally put and negatived. This prevents anyone else moving to reconsider, as he otherwise could at the next meeting, and so makes the vote conclusive.

The principal business was to pass a vote for $300,000 for Street and other Improvements, submitted in a lump sum by the Executive, without details! No one asked for details, but it was moved and carried by 35 to 32 that, instead of a lump sum of $300,000, $16,000 be spent in each of the 25 wards. It was in vain pointed out that this was wasteful and absurd, as the need and size of improvements differed. However, it was freely said in debate that neither the Aldermen nor the Mayor would agree, so that the evening was wasted on a purely academic discussion.

Professor Dewey hoped that "within another decade," Boston would succeed in abolishing the farcical parody on popular representative government.

❪*May 22nd.*

Left Boston with regret. The Fairchilds, with whom we stayed the greater part of the time, were an attractive family. The mother had been uncommonly good looking and had the dignified graciousness of the elderly American lady. The daughter—Sally Fairchild—a tall, graceful girl with "brilliant" hair, pretty features and a bright and capable intelligence, was remarkable in having combined personal charm with a semi-professional career as teacher in primary schools.

The sons still in the student stage, were well-mannered, though not interesting, excepting one who was to be a musician. A gloom had settled over the family. The father was, I gather, a feckless individual, who had lost a large fortune and lived away from his family in New York, trying, without success, to retrieve his fortune. As the Fairchilds were among *The families* in Boston, many attractive persons dropped in to welcome their guests. Judge Wendall [Oliver Wendell] Holmes, the Lowells, the Adams and others—good-looking and cultivated persons—perhaps somewhat "over-trained" but actually engaged in the Law and administration of their own States. Sidney addressed a select company of Boston folk at the 20th Century Club: also a meeting of the members of the Unpaid Boards and the Mayor's Advisory Committee—a meeting summoned by Mayor Quincy to meet us. These men and women were first-rate citizens—in the main, shrewd men of business, together with a few from the academic and "good society" sets. I gathered from talking to them that they felt their position somewhat anomalous; they were uncertain whether they were counsellors or tools —whether they actually modified the working of the municipal machine or whether they were simply being used to represent it favourably to enlightened public opinion. I should imagine that Quincy, with his calculating cool-headedness, used his unpaid Board and Advisory Committee to check the clamouring of War politicians and used the Ward politicians as an excuse for not taking the advice of the representatives of enlightened public opinion—making, in short, the best of both worlds.

The last evening we spent listening to a "Hearing!" Quincy was giving to a Trade Union case. A man in the Electrical Department had been dismissed by the Superintendent for intriguing against him in order to get his place. The Central Labour Union (Trade Council) of which the deplaced man was President took up the case and insisted on being represented by counsel. It was an unsavoury business. The plaintiff was a handsome Irishman, with a thoroughly vicious expression; the counsel was a low attorney; the Committee were what we should call in England a "scratch lot"—unpleasant faces and bad manners. The Superintendent, an inferior weak-looking individual was totally unable to put his own case with plausibility. He stated that he had joined the Electrical Union in order to smooth matters in the Department: that the discharged foreman had begged him to dismiss six other union men whom he (the foreman) declared to be incompetent. After the Superintendent had dismissed these men on the foreman's advice the foreman instigated the men to bring charges against the Superintendent within the Union so as to get him turned out and the Union men withdrawn from the Department. The conspiracy was practically admitted by the plaintiff's lawyer (but it was urged that every man tried to oust his superior and that so long as the plaintiff had not disobeyed orders and had done his work there was no ground for dismissal). This glimpse of the inner workings of a department rather confirmed our impression that the municipal administration is somewhat rotten at its base. But then the base is Irish!

Mayor Quincy interested us, not only on account of his somewhat remarkable personality, but because his career is typical of American politics. A Democrat in a Republican State, he is for practical purposes restricted to a Municipal Government under the dominion of his own Party. The customary residential qualifications effectually shut him out of Congress seeing that he can represent no other State or even district than the one he lives in. Owing to the strong feeling in favour of rotation of office he can only take part in municipal administration for short intervals. He cannot, for instance, be Mayor for more than four years. And the centralisation of all effective power in the Executive and the complete degradation of the Representative Assembly, renders service on the Board of Aldermen or Common Council of no account. When Quincy leaves the Mayoralty his political career is in all probability ended. There are two possible opportunities open to him. He might be selected by a Democratic President for Cabinet office at Washington. Or, by an extraordinary stroke of fortune, he might find himself Democratic candidate for the Presidency itself! Meanwhile the complete absorption of his energies in the office of Mayor—his identification with the political machine—the growth of the habits and temper of an autocrat—all these circumstances damage him for making his way in any profession. By its strange constitution, the U.S.A. offers no permanent work or livelihood to its politicians or administrators, whilst it utterly unfits them for all other professions. No wonder the best men refuse to "enter in." The only way to make a really good job of an administrative or political career in America would be to alternate it with literary or scientific work. But this, besides demanding peculiar qualifications, means considerable independent means.

❨[*May 24th.*

From Yale—a pretty little conventional University—we journeyed via New York to Pittsburg so as to see an American "industrial centre". As a city it is a veritable purgatory. The streets are dark, narrow, badly paved, combining all the turmoil of American cars and pushing citizens with the noxious smells of an old Italian city. There is a dead weight of smoke-laden air that would disgrace the Black country: row on row of wooden shanties, in disreputable repair, climb the steep hills, which surround the city, in an anarchic fashion, without reason or design: whilst the narrow basin into which the business part of the town is situated consists of towering offices, crowding out from all light and air, streets of shabby tenement houses. On the other side of the river are the huge works—steel and glass, belching forth volumes of the blackest smoke. Only one good feature—a noble court house and prison, designed by Richardson—a monument of gloomy silent dignity, dominating this squalid city.[4]

A sharp looking young fellow—aged about 30—clean-shaven and neatly turned out, with easy self-assured address, called in the morning to escort us round Homestead. He was the superintendant of the store department—the buyer of the old steel, the new machinery, the bricks and all the other requisites for the Carnegie Works (they own their own ore and coal). He was a shrewd commonplace young man, with a devouring zeal to get rich, an untiring loyalty to the Carnegie firm and an unbounden admiration for such of the Carnegie partners who having achieved wealth retire to Florida or Europe and have "a good time." From him we gathered that the firm is controlled by a committee of nine, eight of the managers and H. A. [Henry Clay] Frick who acts as chairman and is one of the principal proprietors. Besides the

---

4. Mrs. Webb expanded upon her distaste for Pittsburgh in a personal letter: "Pittsburg is a veritable Hell of a place: a city which combines the smoke & dirt of the worst part of the Black Country with the filthy drainage system of the most archaic Italian city. The people are a God-forsaken lot: rents about half as much again as the most crowded slums of London, tenements built back to back—crazy wooden structures crammed in between offices 20 stories high, streets narrow & crowded with electric trains rushing through at 20 miles an hour—altogether a most diabolic place with the corruptest of corrupt American governments" (Beatrice Webb to Kate Courtney, Chicago, May 29, 1898). Charles Philips Trevelyan had visited Pittsburgh ahead of the Webbs and told them what to expect: "It is another Newcastle, Manchester, Bradford for smoke and grime. But it is chaos municipally. The tram service is bad, and in the hands of corporations. The inclined railways would never be passed by the Bd of Trade, and are in the hands of Corporations. A toll is levied on every one of the four bridges over to Allegheny, the Salford of this Manchester, and they are in the hands of Corporations. The City government is as corrupt as it can be, and it is in the hands of Corporations. The streets are so bad that except along . . . the main streets you could not bicycle at all. There is a great deal of tenement property in the centre of the town. On the hills of the nearer suburbs apparently anyone plants his house where he pleases without reference to roads or public authorities. The reform movement is beginning, at present in not a very effective way. Carnegie and the millionaires have given a Park or two, a free library or so and a score of organs. Otherwise, they leave the city severely alone" (Charles Philips Trevelyan to Beatrice Webb, Chicago, April 19, 1898).

supreme inner executive there is a council of superintendents, presided over by the president of the corporation. This
large body—consisting of about 25—is consultative only; it
meets once a week, has a sumptuous lunch and discusses
business, each man offering suggestions with regard to his
own department. All these superintendents have an interest
in the concern; our young man had been recently admitted
to this advisory council. The policy of the firm has always
been to keep the management *youthful.* When a man reaches
45 he is supposed to retire, or at any rate to become merely
a "consultant." All executive officers should be under 45 so
that Carnegie's great works are not ruled by one-man power,
but by committees of co-operating experts all young and
keenly interested in promoting the growth of the concern.
And one can well imagine, that with a substantial income
during the years of effort and the prospect of retiring with
a large fortune at 45 there is little inducement to the managers or superintendents to accept bribes or be otherwise
than "straight" in their dealings with the firm. One notices
too, a lavishness towards all the brain-workers; the firm providing them with elegant homes, giving them outings to
Europe, and endless treatings at home. Another advantage
of this kind of business organisation is the absence of outside
shareholders clamouring for dividends on the existing capital. The proprietors all being working members of the firm
earning high salaries, the surplus profits each year can be
spent on extending the works and improving the mechanical
contrivances. We were told both by our young man and
afterwards by Frick, that they never hesitated to tear up and
demolish any of the plant if they thought a new plant would
pay handsomely *on the new capital to be expended.* The
value of the old plant was simply written off. It is said that
Carnegie's works replace all their plant every three years.
It is, I think, to this lavish generosity towards their brain-
workers and stimulus to their co-operative energies com-

bined with this extravagant expenditure, on improvements, that the Carnegie business owes its rapid and phenominal success.

Towards labour they have acted for the last six years in a niggardly and oppressive fashion. They have abolished trade unionism throughout all their works—steel, coke, and mines and railways. They employ labourers for twelve hours a day at 5/- (the rent of a slum tenement being 8/- a week, and if an artisan's house, £1) * all other commodities dear in proportion. They show no concern for the comfort, safety or education of their workpeople; they seem, in fact, to be the worst kind of sweaters. Consequently their firm has an evil reputation in the labour world, and their mines and coke ovens are said, even by their fellow capitalists, to be worked by the scum of the country. And if one regards the effect on the character of the brainworkers as of any consequence, Carnegie's works are a potent agent in demoralising the governing classes of their own community. These 30 or 40 eager young men, who run the concern, have their whole energies absorbed in money making; they have as the ideal before them the lives of Mr. Carnegie and Mr. Frick—men who directly they have made their pile, leave Pittsburg and, to use the words of our young guide, "entertain finely in Paris and London." Not a member of the firm has any connection with the federal, state or municipal government. It is only another aspect of this kind of capitalism, that the state of Pennsylvania and the city of Pittsburg are so abjectly corrupt that state and city have become bye-words, even among American politicians.

We followed our young friend through acres of shops filled with the most powerful and newest machinery. The place seemed almost deserted by human beings.† The great engines, cranes and furnaces were struggling and panting,

* The £1 includes the use of water and natural gas and fuel.
† Frick told us that they employ about 3,000 men in steel manufacture, but though they had increased their output threefold they had decreased their employment of labour by 400 in the last few years.

seemingly without the aid of man. It was only now and again that one espied a man enclosed in a little cabin, swinging midway between the ground and the rafts of the shed, and working some kind of electrical machine whereby millions of horse power was set in motion and directed. Or here and there one noticed a sullen looking figure watching through blue spectacles the heated metal of the converters. With the quick sensitiveness of the American our self-assured young man perceived that in spite of our polite phrases of admiration we were not altogether impressed with this vast wealth-producing machine and the "fine time" which it was grinding out for its directors. "Mr. Frick is a fine gentleman: he entertains splendidly at Paris—all the artists of Europe— and he has such an elegant home" he reiterated, with a certain growing uneasiness. "And he takes no interest in the municipal affairs of Pittsburg?" I asked with a polite but cold intonation. The young man looked at us with a certain astonishment and hurriedly said "That is our weak point, Mrs. Webb, our rich men are not interested in public affairs: they leave that to men who can't succeed in business—poor sort of living, and even then uncertain. Oh! My! I would not care to be a politician."

Later in the day we saw Mr. Frick. He was just a commonplace business man: somewhat untidy in dress and with the pronunciation and language of an uncultivated shopkeeper. Not that he was in any way repulsive: he had good features and kindly expression, and the usual courtesy of the American. But he answered our questions with a certain uneasiness and was, I think, relieved when we departed.

(
(*Entry in S. W.'s handwriting*)
We were told by our young friend (McGrew), by Frick, and by another managing partner whom he summoned to inform us, that the firm preferred to educate its own managers, superintendents and generally all persons in authority. They

were taken in as boys, with the usual common school education, and promoted according to their merits with extraordinary rapidity. All those in authority were admitted into partnership—McGrew and four others had been taken in this year, making a total of 34 shareholders only, possessing this capital of eleven millions sterling (55 million dollars), all accumulated out of the profits of the concern. Frick said that McGrew (a distant connection of his own) was allotted one-ninth of one per cent, equal to $50,000. This he had to pay for—that is, the amount was debited against him, and he was charged interest on it, the assumption being that the dividends credited on this stock would not merely cover the interest due, but also very rapidly wipe out the debit.

Chemists and metallurgists are taken from technical schools, largely the Boston Institute of Technology; and civil engineers from that at Troy, N.Y. But here again youth and Carnegie education are desired, these scientific experts being always taken immediately on graduation, at 19 or 21. There had also, by exception, been a few young Swedes, of scientific education in Sweden. But complete reliance was now placed on American science, and the education which the works themselves afforded. We did not gather that the scientific men enjoyed any great consideration, or that they took the leading part in the administration—Carnegie, Frick and Phipps—the three principal people, has been business men only. Carnegie, son of a poor Scotch weaver, made his first capital by a lucky speculation in mineral oil land, and started the steel works about 1865, at the close of the war.[5] We gathered that the great technological advances in labour-saving had been made in the past ten years, largely in the application of electric power to

5. Soon after their return to England, the Webbs' friend Richard Burdon Haldane, Lord Haldane of Cloan, consulted with them about approaching Carnegie for an endowment of the University of London. Having seen Pittsburgh and having a low opinion of Carnegie—Mrs. Webb referred to him as "the reptile"—they refused to approach him directly, but Mr. Webb agreed to draft a description of what might be done (Barbara Drake and Margaret I. Cole, eds., *Our Partnership, by Beatrice Webb* [London, 1948], pp. 185–86).

work new automatic machinery. The "travelling buggies"
which replaced labour in moving the great masses of steel in
and out of the rolling mills; the automatic machinery by which
a single man swinging on a moving arm, opened the furnace
door, lifted out the heated mass of steel, and swung it on to
the buggy; and the automatic charging of the furnaces them-
selves with cradles of scrap steel also by a single man, were all
introduced within the last six years.

❲*May 29th.*
Two days at Cincinnati—well spent. [M. E.] Ingalls, President of the Big Four Railway took charge of us. He is the
best type of American corporation official—a kindly-natured
man with broad statesmanlike views. He is open-minded to
new ideas, but shrewdly aware of the ends *he* wishes to promote, namely the prosperity of the Big Four and his own
personal power. A Democrat in politics he threw himself,
with all his might, on to the other side in the 1896 election,
thinking that free silver meant commercial disaster. And it
was largely to his influence that organised labour was roped
in by the Republicans, the rank and file being persuaded that
silver meant higher prices and lower wages, whilst the officials were not only intellectually converted but promised
their share of the spoils. Hence [Terence V.] Powderly was
taken into McKinley's administration and the general secretary of the steel workers was only the other day made customs officer at Pittsburg. Ingalls is an optimist with regard
to the future of America. He believes that in all industries
which depend on perfection of mechanical contrivances
America will beat the world. "Where you English excel" he
cheerfully admitted "and will apparently continue to excel,
is in manufactures which demand human patience and human skill—and in all trading which requires a good and a
long credit. The integrity of the English commercial world
is splendid" added the American railway king with cheery

sympathy. "So long as the Englishman feels confident that he will get his money in the end he does not care how long he waits for it. We are too impatient, we want immediate returns, and we are far too smart, we are not trusted like your men are. The English and Americans are destined to rule the world." This mutual admiration brought about by the so-called Anglo-American alliance lends a pleasant flavour to our intercourse with this emotional people.

One gathers that there is a lack of capital in the majority of enterprises; Ingalls stating that it was impossible for his railway to raise sufficient to carry on the express business (for passenger luggage) or to run its own Pullman Cars. The question arises, what is the effect, on national prosperity, of capital being shovelled into concerns like Carnegie's, and doled out, with extreme meagreness, to other undertakings? Generally speaking Ingalls believes in the American institutions: he is, for instance, enthusiastic about the present condition of the House of Representatives under Speaker Reed's domination. "The House gives us no trouble: it is the Senate that is always upsetting things: Reed is the greatest American of his time." He admits however that there are two black spots; the American system of taxation and American municipal institutions. He is one of the few capitalists who are strongly in favour of an income tax: thinks that at present the rich escape their fair burden, and that this fraud on their side will inevitably lead to dangerous reactions in taxation (just as Carnegie's treatment of labour will lead to dangerous re-action in the direction of hampering corporations). Ingalls in fact has the English attitude towards political questions: he believes in giving way wherever there is a grievance; even a sentimental grievance; rather than stamping opposition out, misled by the notion that you must resist the beginnings of changes. As for municipal government, he thinks there has been an improvement in net results though municipal morality is still very low.

He treated us with the usual lavish American kindness. He

called on us at our hotel the morning we arrived, arranged for us to lunch with him that day to meet the city auditor to go to the great May festival with his womenkind in the evening. The next day we were to spend on a trolly ride— a special car to traverse the whole electric system of Cincinnati, finishing up with a dinner at his house. His wife and niece were common fat uninteresting women with the infantile ways of rich American women; the beauty of the music made the evening agreeable. The trolly ride was remunerative: for he had invited three or four of the leading Cincinnati citizens—among others Coulster—the railway attorney who had invented government by injunction, the boss of the great book trust. I was so absorbed in talking shop to these two that I hardly noticed the miles of pretty suburbs through which we passed. I utterly failed to make Coulston [Edward Colston] (a Southerner and old confederate army man) understand our objections to the use of injunctions in labour quarrels. It was interesting to note, by the way, that he was using the recent Lords' decision in *Hood v. Allen,* as a precedent in the case of a group of railway companies—for the reversal of the decision of a lower court casting the company in damages for blacklisting one particular man and preventing him from earning his livelihood.

The organiser of the Book Trust was a somewhat coarse grained blatant individual who had just recently removed his nominal residence to Maine in order to escape the tax on personality. Until the trust was formed he had not been assessed, but owing to the notoriety consequent on the formation of the great corporation he found himself assessed on his share in the concern. He had fought the case in the courts but had been beaten and had now removed his home to Maine. He was a thoroughgoing American: believed that the function of congress was to register the will of the majority; believed in rotation of office and in the spoils system and thought the U.S.A. the best of all possible worlds. The Book Trust supplied five-eighths of the school books in the United

States, spent three-quarters of a million dollars annually on agents and their expenses. They are known to bribe school committees and teachers, which accounts for his admitting that American school committees and boards were steadily degrading. During the last ten years these committees and boards have "slipped into politics" to use his phrase.

The municipal government of Cincinnati is just now passing through a convulsion. For many years the State Legislation has been chipping and changing the Cincinnati charter to suit the exigencies of State politics. About 1891 Ingalls and other influential reformers drafted a charter which they thought would settle the matter, vesting the whole government in a bipartisan Board of Administrators appointed by the Mayor. Of course, a powerful Republican Boss—[George B.] Cox—captured the city, appointed his own Mayor, who appointed the Boss's creatures—two Republicans and two Democrats. One of the Republicans—Herman [August Herrmann] by name—was the first lieutenant of the Boss, the other three were mere dummies. Herman ruled the city for seven years with an iron hand. A man of great capacity, he seems to have given the citizens of Cincinnati (from all accounts) a good deal for their money: but meantime he built himself a fine house and his wife appeared in silks and diamonds. The ambition of the Boss meanwhile transcended the city limits: he spread out into the State and began to sell the nominations to the Judgeships. The tampering with the Judiciary alarmed persons of Ingall's temperament; whilst a notable army of opponents in the city was being recruited by the men who failed to get nominated to offices to which they thought they had a right. Into this ferment stepped an old Democratic Boss who desired to become a U.S. Senator in place of Herman. He organised a fusion between Democrats and disaffected Republicans and disapproving Reformers. The city government and city representation in State Legislature was captured by the fusion ticket. A new Charter was forthwith drafted providing for a new "Board of city affairs" having exactly the same functions as the old Board but of course consisting of the nominees of the new Mayor. The legality of this Act on technical grounds was now in dispute in the Supreme Court. It was part of the irony of the event that the Democratic Boss failed to achieve his main end and Herman is still U.S. Senator.[6]

We saw both the "Ins" and the "Outs". The Town Hall was crowded with loafers of all classes, with here and there an old official haunting the corridors and awaiting dismissal. The new Board, appointed under the new Charter, by the new Mayor, was constitutionally bi-partisan, that is to say, the Mayor had to appoint two of each party (in future they were to be elected and would therefore cease to be bi-partisan). We watched their proceedings: an indifferent looking set of men, decent enough but not capable. The chairman was allowing the proceedings to go on in a slipshod fashion: the clerk, who had just had his salary reduced (he could not be removed for a year and they wanted him to resign) was reading letters in a sulky sort of way; the other five members were chattering together, or casually interviewing the swarm of office seekers. One of them passed us the enclosed letter to show the character of their correspondence. We heard the next day that the six members were dismissing old officials right and left, and dividing up the patronage; appointing "heelers" to the city offices. And this was the result of a reform movement!

As we were leaving the Council Chamber the stenographer, a bright managing woman, beckoned us into her office. She was not going to be removed because the Editors of the two party papers said she was not to be. She felt, therefore, free to express her opinion of her new masters, which was discreetly "sniffy." "You must see Mr. Herman: he really knows the city business. He is now President of the

6. Mrs. Webb was confused here. No one named Herman or Herrmann was ever United States Senator from Ohio. Ohio's Senators in 1898 were Marcus Alonzo Hanna and Joseph B. Foraker. Foraker was from Cincinnati.

Water Commission: I will introduce you to him tomorrow."
"He will be back here in three weeks' time—I reckon."

The interview came off. Herman was a suspicious, sinister-looking individual, unwieldy and almost bloated in form, with heavy sensual face, square forehead and eyes sloping Chinese fashion upwards from the nose. But he looked a forceful able man, not a speaker or popular leader, but an organizer and administrator. And certainly he did know the city's business. To him the city was a great Corporation to be run, on business principles, with just as much attention to the "heeler" as was necessary to keep the Party in power. He was, of course "moderate" in his policy; against the city owning or working monopolies or services, against the fair wages clauses, in favour of rigid economy and "no fads." I can well believe even his enemies' report that the city under his administration had got its money's worth. If he could get a "cut" off the corporations' or contractors' necessary profits, what did it matter to the citizens, he would say. He gave us excellent details on paper of the facts of his administration. From all we saw the Cincinnati Government of the last seven years was an excellent example of "government by syndicate." "The new Board" admitted Ingalls "will either give us less service or charge us more money. If Cox had not tampered with the State judiciary we should not have meddled with his government of the City. The revolt with regard to the city affairs" he added "was largely a matter of sentiment: the citizens did not like to see Herman and Cox bursting out into large houses and expensive entertainments when Cox had no salary and Herman only 5,000 dollars a year. It annoyed us."

All the same I don't believe, if the Democratic Boss had *not* wished to be Senator, there would have been a new charter or Board of City affairs.

part **II** *June 1–July 10*

¶*June 1st, 1898—Chicago.*

Exhausting journey from Cincinnati in the heat, after a morning of interviewing: Arrived at the house of the Zeublins [Zueblins] dead tired late in the evening.

¶*June 11th—Denver*

Our visit to Chicago was unfortunate. In the first four days Sidney sickened with bad sore throat and fever and was prostrate; I followed suit after he had recovered and am still suffering from the remnants of the disease. Hence our vision of Chicago has been blurred by ill health and anxiety. The home of the Zeublins, close to the University, was attractive. Professor [Charles] Zeublin is a Fabian who has been much in England: a sympathetic pleasant person, well favoured in body and mind, and with eclectic information on political questions. He is of the type of University Extension lecturer —neither a litterateur nor a scientific man; just a cultivated right-minded individual who has a facile tongue and agreeable manner. His wife, a prim and pretty little New Englander, is shrewder than she looks, and as good company as

her husband. They lived on the "outskirts" of the University
in more ways than one. But we gathered that this bran new
place of learning (the result of Rockefeller's generosity) is
without form. Dr. [William Rainey] Harper, the President,
pushes all he knows how to secure a permanent foundation.
Not to commit himself on any question is his settled policy. While staying with the Zeublins we saw the Professors
[J. Lawrence] Laughlin (individualist economist), [Albion
W.] Small, Van Holst [Hermann E. von Holst], [Frank Jus-
tus] Miller, [Charles Richmond] Henderson and others—Van
Holst, the only man of mark: but he belongs to a German
University of fifty years ago: no new suggestions on political
or economic questions. Altogether grown barren.

Lunched with Robert Lincoln, now Chairman of Pullman
Co; formerly ambassador in London. Commonplace philistine
American, with a certain brutal strength, possibly with some
administrative capacity, but, I should think, floated on his
father's reputation into a position of importance. He had the
ill-humour of continuous over-feeding and over-drinking: the
hard uninspired intelligence of a complete materialist. His
womenkind were just the common rich type without intellectual curiosity or public spirit. Mrs. Lincoln said she had
never felt so completely satisfied and at home as in London
Society. Hard on London Society! The married daughter who
had brought the sole heir to the Lincoln wealth into the
world—congratulated her odious little son, across the table,
on being able to call in his friends whenever he wanted them
and "to send them away whenever he felt inclined." The
other daughter has eloped and been disowned. Altogether an
unlovely household. Lincoln had nothing to say of interest.

Lunched with Ex-Governor [John Peter] Altgeld, to whom
Leonard Courtney gave us an introduction. Leonard had
been sympathetic to the Bryan campaign and Altgeld was
most anxious to be helpful.

The first impression of Altgeld when he called after dinner
at the Zeublins was disappointing. A cross between a work-

man and a dissenting minister: I should have said if he had
been English. In dress and general bearing a dissenting minister; in his slow literal speech a workingman unaccustomed
to conversation. One expected personal dignity and a certain
"savoir faire" in a Governor who has made all America ring
with his name.

When we lunched with him I listened to his account of
his past life and of his political experiences, and watched his
changing expression. A strong independent will and self ret-
icent manner; a man who is clearly not to be intimidated or
put into the background by anyone. His mouth is firm, but
his grey eyes have a curious visionary expression, a far off
look as if he were always testing his opinions by some abstract reasoning. There is no American shrewdness, no quick
perception of men; theory dominates his life and he is impatient of expediency. What makes him to my mind a dangerous ruler of men is the complete absence of tradition (inherited experience) and of science (present experience). He
is a metaphysician and not a statesman.

We asked him about current American problems. All we
could discover was a basis of Jeffersonian individualism and
a superstructure of half accepted German Collectivism. He
had no idea of an organic society, no vision of the need for
the expert, or even for the representative. Any just man could
administer justice; it was good for all citizens to take their
turn at governing others; it was bad for any man to be too
long in power, for power corrupted the heart of man. *Therefore* the cure for all American evils was the election of the
judges of the Supreme Court by the whole people and for
one term only. And they were to be ineligible for re-election!
He believed every question could be settled by a guileless
reference to some undisputed first principle to which all
good men would agree. He was not the skilled brainworker:
he was the skilled maker of things, brooding magnificently
in his leisure about ultimate principles, speaking weighty
words to his fellow workmen, exciting them to discontent. He

confessed, with obvious sincerity, that the part of his life he was proudest of was not his career as Governor of a State but the building of a block of offices twenty storeys high. It had been a relief to him to get rid of his complicated work of Government.[7]

⟪

(Entry in S. W.'s handwriting)

The government of Chicago, which as far as results are concerned, seems to reach the lowest depths of municipal inefficiency, is, in form, rather of an old type. The charter in force dates from 1870, though it has been much modified by special legislation. There is a single legislative council, of 68 "Aldermen" elected by 34 wards; and in this Council the Mayor presides (the only instance of this English practice that we have come across). But the Mayor seems to exercise no official influence in the Council. He does not, for instance, nominate the Committees, nor is he ex-officio or otherwise a member of them. (By exception, one special committee on the Elevation of Railroad Tracks, is always nominated by the Mayor, and he sits on it). The Mayor gets $10,000 a year ($7,000 down to 1897), and seems, for all his presiding over the Council, to fill the ordinary place of an American mayor, viz. the chief executive officer. He appoints all the heads of departments who are not directly elected (these latter are the Treasurer,

7. Mrs. Webb reiterated her misgivings about Altgeld in a letter to one of her sisters: "Tell the Courtneys that we saw a good deal of Ex Governor Altgeld. He is an attractive man with a strong independent will and a visionary intellect—with neither traditions nor any great knowledge of men or affairs. I am not sure that I do not think him a *dangerous* fellow: he reasons from abstract principles of the Jeffersonian type with little respect for either present facts or past experience" (Beatrice Webb to Mary Playne, Denver, June 10, 1898). Trevelyan, however, did not share her opinion of Altgeld: "I had several talks with Altgeld who is the ablest man I have met yet in the States, rather dour but a good companion at bottom. [Henry Demerest] Lloyd too is very interesting. They are the two men you must not miss" (Charles Philips Trevelyan to Sidney Webb, St. Louis, May 2, 1898). Apparently the Webbs did not meet Lloyd.

City Clerk, City Attorney); and the principal officers so appointed (viz. the Commissioner of Public Works, the Corporation Counsel, Comptroller and Chief of Police) are said to form the Mayor's Cabinet.

By the way, Washburn [Hempstead Washburne], a recent Mayor, refused to preside over the Council, and confined himself to his Executive duties. Nothing happened except that the Council appointed a President of its own pro-tem.

The Council appoints its Committees by party caucus of the dominant majority, which puts on only such of the minority as it chooses. This, too, is the only instance of this kind that we have found (not counting the U.S. Senate). At present in the Chicago Council the Republicans are 30 to 38 Democrats; and the much more important cross-division of honest men versus corrupt is about the same (30 to 38). As some of the honest Democrats refused to coalesce with the Republicans, honest and dishonest, at the outset of this new Council, the Democratic majority, mostly dishonest, packed the committees to its liking, putting on the committees a very small proportion of Republicans at all, and steadfastly excluding all honest Republicans (and also indeed all Democrats who could not be relied upon to vote without reference to honesty) from all but unimportant committees. Thus, though the reformers this Spring so far gained a partial victory at the polls—for Chicago has not within living memory had so large a minority reputed honest—yet that minority is powerless in the Council, save only that it is large enough to prevent any vote being passed over the Mayor's veto.

When we visited the Council we found the usual disorderly procedure—members smoking freely in spite of a Standing Rule expressly forbidding it; no agenda of any kind; everything read by a reading clerk; voting by call of ayes and nays and members rising to "explain their vote" after the vote had been taken: constant talking among the members, and between them and the visitors "on the floor;" and all the swinging of chairs, opening and shutting of desks, reading of newspapers and writing of letters that marks American public bodies from those at Washington downwards.

As we entered, "Bathhouse John" [John Coughlin], a saloon and private bathkeeper, and leading ward politician, was bawling at the top of his voice in Hyde Park style, reciting a flamboyant resolution denouncing any alliance between the U.S. and England on the ground that England had persistently oppressed all weaker nationalities from Ireland to the natives everywhere; that America had beaten her when America had but three millions of people, and had no need of her now that there were seventy millions; that they were not Anglo Saxons but Americans, and so forth. His claim of urgency for this resolution was lost on the vote, and it was, after another vote, referred to the Committee on the Judiciary! The whole thing was taken as a joke of Bathhouse John's.

It should be stated that the Council had got so far as to have distributed among the Aldermen a type-written list of the improvements they were to vote that evening (pavement, sewers &c. in various streets), and these were all voted en bloc without a word, each Alderman being allowed practically to put in the list whatever he pleased for his own ward.

These "improvements" (which with us would be the ordinary government) are charged, by way of special assessment, upon the owners of the property in the streets in question, and are not, in practice, even undertaken until a majority of the property owners along the street petition for them. Thus whether a Chicago street shall be paved or not, whether its sidewalks shall be of rotting planks or stone, whether its roadway shall be dirt, or wood, or brick or asphalt, is made to depend on a vote of the property owners, largely little property-owners, in the street affected, the vote being in all cases biassed by the feeling of the property-owners, not only that they will be mulcted in an indefinite sum for the "improvement," but also by the well-grounded suspicion that the Aldermen of the Ward and the Contractors will all get their picking out of the *job.* When a pavement wears out, as is constantly happening, the mere relaying of the pavement is deemed an "improvement" of this kind. Add to this the fact that it is usual to throw all the burden of keeping the pavement in repair on the Contractors for a long term, often 5 years; that the whole administration is so corrupt that no one sees that the Contractor lays the pavement decently in the first instance, still less dreams of enforcing his liability to keep in repair—and the reason why the Chicago pavements are bad becomes clear enough.

And the pavements are unspeakably bad! The sidewalks uneven and dilapidated even when of stone in the busy streets, are nothing but rotten planks in the slum streets, with great holes rendering it positively dangerous to walk in the dark. The roadways in the crowded business streets are, at best, of the roughest cobbles, most unevenly laid, with great holes and prominances. In the slum streets they are usually made of wood—not wood pavement as we know it, squared blocks on concrete—but merely round slices of tree-stems, placed on a dirt surface. This instantly wears uneven, and the unjoined circles of soft wood lie about loose on the mud. Imagine on sidewalks and roadways of this sort, the garbage and litter of some of the most crowded slums in the world, in an atmosphere as moist and as smoky as our Black Country towns, unswept, unwashed, untended from year's end to year's end. On the edge of the sidewalk are "garbage-boxes" large uncovered receptacles, loosely built of unjoined planks, for decaying vegetable matter, which is left to putrefy in the open air until the city's carts come round to empty it.

This utter inefficiency of municipal government so far as the streets are concerned is partly explained by the absurd state of the City's finances. The tax levied by the Council is limited by the Illinois State Constitution to 2 per cent of the assessed capital value of property. But the assessment is left to the tender mercy of one assessor, elected by the district which he assesses. As there are eight such districts in the city,

and no check and no sort of machinery for keeping the districts
level, each assessor does his best to keep his own district as
low as possible, and usually reduces the total below what it
was when he came in. The result of this competition of assessors as to which of them can bring his district down lowest,
is that the valuation of Chicago to-day, with 1¾ million inhabitants, is less than it was in 1867, when the population was
¼ million. In the last six years, it has fallen by more than 10
per cent whilst the population has risen by over 25%. (This
system is just being changed; a Board of Assessors to be elected
by the whole city; with an appeal to a Board of Review, of
three persons also elected by the whole city.)

The result is that the City Council and the Mayor can only
levy about eight shillings per head in taxes for all their purposes. If it were not for the fact that they get nearly as much
again from other sources,—mostly from saloon licenses—the
City would be quite bankrupt. As it is, this City of 1¾ inhabitants spends only £30,000 a year on street pavement re-
pairs for all its 180 square miles, and only £120,000 a year on
street cleaning.

The only decent municipal enterprise (beyond the Fire
Department which is good in all American cities and may
therefore be good even in Chicago), is the great system of
parks and connecting boulevards. There are three Park Commissions, two appointed by the Governor of the State, and one
by the Judges—the latter odd way of constructing a municipal
body being said to produce the most efficient body. The parks
are excellently laid out and kept, those on the South Side in
particular, under the Judge-made Commission. This body carries to an extreme the principle of Direct Employment, even
running successfully by its own servants, the park restaurants,
where municipal ice-cream and other viands are sold. The
boulevards between the parks are sometimes broad stretches
of green with avenues sometimes merely an asphalted street
through the heart of the city. Thus, Jackson Boulevard is only
a street running from West Chicago to the Lake. It was

handed over to the Park Commission, and accepted by them, merely as an expedient for getting it paved with asphalt, the necessary outburst of public opinion having been largely supplied by the bicyclists of Chicago. The expenses of the Park Commission are levied as an extra tax on the several districts graduated according to their assumed benefit.

There is a limit of city debt to two per cent of the assessed value, but the Parks, Schools, Drainage, and Water are outside this limit, and have (narrow) limits of their own. The water supply is managed by a separate Commission appointed by the State Governor. The water is simply pumped up from Lake Michigan, and supplied unfiltered. It is thought a wonderful advance that the intakes are now a mile or two away from the shore, instead of close by as was formerly the case.

The drainage of the City is supposed to be diverted from the lake, and sent down a canalised river into the Mississippi (crude).

It should be added that Chicago has, as a city, practically no "Public Charities," these being done by Cook County, of which the city forms the greater part. The schools are under a Board of Education of 21 members, appointed by the Mayor, 7 retiring annually. There is also a separate Board for the Public Library, appointed in like manner.

The citizen of Chicago, in addition to his 2 per cent to the City Council, pays separate taxes to Cook County and Illinois State, and separate taxes also for the Parks, Drainage, Water and Library Commissions—amounting altogether to 8 or 10 per cent of the valuation (capital). But, all told, he pays (as far as I can make out) only about 32/- per head, as against at least twice as much per head in London, where all work cost much less.

On the Thursday, after our arrival at Chicago, we migrated from the attractive home of the Zeublins, surrounded by green lawns and avenues of trees, down to Hull House Settle-

ment in the very heart of Chicago slums. Hull House itself
is a spacious mansion, with all its rooms opening, American
fashion, into each other. There are no doors, or, more exactly,
no *shut* doors: the residents wander from room to room,
visitors wander here, there and everywhere; the whole
ground floor is, in fact, one continuous passage leading no-
where in particular. The courtyard, in front of the house, is
always filled with slum children. At the back, opening out of
the kitchen, is a rough and ready restaurant. There is the
usual scanty service; the front door being answered by the
resident who happens, at that time, to be nearest to it.

The residents consist, in the main, of strong-minded energetic women, bustling about their various enterprises and
professions, interspersed with earnest-faced self-subordinat-
ing and mild-mannered men who slide from room to room
apologetically. One continuous intellectual and emotional
ferment is the impression left on the visitor to Hull House.

Miss Jane Addams, the Principal, is without doubt a remarkable woman, an interesting combination of the organiser, the enthusiast and the subtle observer of human characteristics. Her article in the *International Journal of Ethics*
—"Ethical Survivals in Municipal Corruption" is an exact
analysis of the forces of Tammany organisation and its root
in human nature. She has a charming personality, gentle and
dignified, shrewdly observant: above all she excels in per-
sistency of purpose and unflinching courage. She has made
Hull House; and it is she who has created whatever spirit of
reform exists in Chicago.

In the evening of our arrival we underwent a terrific or-
deal. First an uncomfortable dinner, a large party served,
higgledepiggledy. Then a stream of persons, labour, municipal, philanthropic, university, all those queer, well-intentioned or cranky individuals, who habitually centre round
all settlements! Every individual among them must needs be
introduced to us (a diabolical custom from which we have
suffered greatly in America). Gradually the crowd pressed

us into a large hall, with chairs for some hundreds and a small platform. From this place, Sidney and I were expected to orate to the assembly, on any topic we chose. We did our best and they were so far entertained, that they asked us innumerable questions.

For a right down exhausting business commend me to a dinner and a reception, preceding a lecture and a severe heckling. However, we seemed to give satisfaction.

The other days of our stay at Hull House are so associated in my memory with sore throat and fever, with the dull heat of the slum, the unappetising food of the restaurant, the restless movements of the residents from room to room, the rides over impossible streets littered with unspeakable garbage, that they seem like one long bad dream lightened now and again by Miss Addams' charming grey eyes and gentle voice and graphic power of expression. We were so completely done up that we settled "to cut" the other cities we had hoped to investigate, Omaha, St. Paul, Minneapolis and Madison; and come straight on here to the restful mountains.[8]

8. The Webbs did not express much regret about having to omit part of their proposed trip: "Here we are in the middle of the Continent, both of us rather overcome with the American weather. I have just recovered from a mild attack of influenza, and now Beatrice is down with it. This has decided us to 'chuck' the rest of these overgrown, ugly cities, each more corrupt and misgoverned than the last, and to make a bee-line for Colorado. There we shall try to get into the Rocky Mountains for a week or so, going probably to a certain high valley . . . where we can lie on our backs and be quiet" (Sidney Webb to George Bernard Shaw, Chicago, June 5, 1898). Besides missing Madison, the Twin Cities, and Omaha, the Webbs passed up Grinnell College, Iowa, and Lincoln, Nebraska, each of which Trevelyan had urged them to visit. Trevelyan had spent five days at Grinnell and was quite taken with the college, calling it "an ideal rural western university." Trevelyan had gone to Lincoln to talk with Bryan and reported that the Great Commoner "would be delighted" to meet the Webbs. Bryan, Trevelyan wrote, "is not a great man; but a slow-moving, conscientious, vigorous politician. He is too much of a politician, not enough of a statesman. He is very much absorbed in silver, though he is ready to talk about the trusts. But he is not ready for large experiments in nationalization or municipal ownership. Altgeld is the statesman, and he is a big one. Bryan is only a very able advocate" (Charles Philips Trevelyan to Beatrice Webb, May 18, 1898). Mrs. Webb met Bryan in England in November, 1903, and again in July, 1906. Her opinion of Bryan was similar to Trevelyan's (Drake and Cole, eds., *Our Partnership*, pp. 276, 350).

Denver is a pleasant little city situated on the great table land 5,000 feet above the sea, stretching almost imperceptibly downwards for a thousand miles to the level plains of Illinois, Indiana and Ohio. It lies at the foot of the Rocky mountains, perhaps some 15 miles distant from the first granite cliffs; an undulating country well-cultivated with its streams marked out by belts of trees—poplars, willows, limes and sweet smelling shrubs. The city itself is remarkably well-built, no slums, no wood shanties; the principal streets made up of granite offices, brick shops and rough marble public buildings. In the suburbs are innumerable villas of all sizes and forms separated from each other only by green turf with the footway and the road over-shadowed by spreading trees. We settled ourselves in one of these little villas where some half dozen married Americans were escaping the troubles of housekeeping or the expenses of an establishment. The majority of these were ordinary folk: the womenkind well-dressed and pleasant mannered, but utterly empty-headed, the men with just the commonplace insignificance of the ordinary American business man. A Mr. and Mrs. Dickenson turned out however to be agreeable and helpful people. Mrs. Dickenson was a Lovejoy, a woman of sense and breeding, much interested in education, her husband also well-read and well bred, the two somewhat depressed by the loss of the greater part of their income in the last panic of 1893. They were keenly critical of the deficiencies in American municipal institutions and the lack of distinction in the society of an American city. Among all the members of this boarding house, pleasant or unpleasant, there was a restless admiration for Eastern America, an uneasy consciousness of their inferiority to New York, Boston or Philadelphia, a dread of the ridicule of the Eastern newspapers, a desire that their children should have the advantages of "Eastern" education. We found exactly the same feeling among the townspeople we came across: very similar in its nature to the feeling of the Eastern cities towards England. If Denver is a fair sample of the West then the West has as yet developed no civilisation independent of the public opinion, traditions and ideals of the Eastern States.

We had an introduction from Altgeld to the Governor [Alva] Adams of Colorado. We wandered through the "Capitol", a pretentious half-finished building, and with difficulty found the "Governor's office." Two or three men were lounging in the outer office, and with little ceremony we were ushered into the Governor's private room. The Governor, a pleasant genial little man with broad shoulders, bullet-shaped head, bushy moustache and kindly grey eyes, rose from his desk and welcomed us cordially. "I thought it was about time you came. I was just reading Governor Altgeld's letter." We straight away opened our enquiry into the details of State Government. But the little man, though most anxious to be helpful, was too uncultivated and muddle-headed to be able to answer our questions with any accuracy or fullness. Moreover, every third minute the alarm of the telephone sounded and with an "excuse me" the Governor took down the receiver from the corner of the desk and entered into a lively conversation with someone in a neighbouring town. (The interruptions of the telephone seem to us to waste half the life of the ordinary American engaged in public or private business: he has seldom half an hour consecutively at his own disposal—a telephone is a veritable *time scatterer*). He explained afterwards that he was tied to his desk because he felt he could not delegate any part of his function. "I can't sleep at night if I have left anything to be decided by my subordinates" said the good little fellow. "Just now I am up to my eyes in work about this war: the President has called up four companies; I want to send twelve: all the best youths in the State are volunteering, the sons of people like you and I, young fellows throwing up places worth $10,000 a year." "In all that concerns the State, you see," he said in answer to some rather involved question of mine, "I am supreme so long as my term lasts. The Legislature only meets once in two years and is limited to ninety days. I can call them up for a special session: but then they can only consider questions which I lay before them. But I can't imagine a man even if he started bad, abusing a position of responsibility and trust like that of the Governor. The very fact that he calls no man master should make him do his duty. The President at Washington has not anything like the same power: at Washington it is *Congregational* Government" explained our unlettered administrator. "People talk about the Supreme Court holding Congress in check, that's all nonsense, Congress can always add to the Supreme Court men who will do what is expected of them," he shrewdly added. "You want to see the municipal council; I'll go down with you now: glad to get out of this office. At this desk I am bound to listen to every man's complaint."

So off we went with the Governor in the Car to the Town Hall. No one in the cars seemed to recognise him; and at the Town Hall, though the officials were friendly, they did not treat him with any particular respect. We sauntered into the Mayor's office, a common shrewd man of Scotch descent, with a young Englishman as private secretary, and an Englishman as stenographer. The Town Hall was as unkempt and dirty as usual: the Board of Aldermen (15 lower chamber members elected by Wards; the "supervisors" 5 members elected at large being the upper chamber) was in session in the corner of a great barrack-like hall. The Mayor [T. S. Mc-Murray] introduced the Governor and ourselves and we sat for half an hour or so listening to the usual routine according to American standing orders: clerk reading out word by word reports of Committees; interjections from members, roll calling, speeches in the middle of the vote being taken; individual members meanwhile smoking, reading, chatting and sleeping, etc. The individuals were an unkempt but decent looking set, mostly working men and small dealers I should think. There was a marked absence of the Ward politician type—a general appearance of inefficiency rather than of dishonesty or coarseness. We gathered from the Mayor that Denver was in the throes of a constitutional revolution. Prior to 1885 the charter gave the Mayor the power to appoint the Fire and Police Board and the Board of Public Works. In that year the citizens thought they could better matters by placing the power of appointment in the hands of the Governor so as to keep the administration of these important offices "out of city politics" and a new charter was engineered through the Legislature. Now they had repented themselves of this abdication of self-government, and were agitating for a new Charter! A convention had been nominated by the Mayor and had its second session that very evening. In spite of our fatigue (my throat was still very bad) we decided to attend this charter-making convention, a type of American meeting we had not yet observed.

The convention met in the same ramshackle hall and occupied the Aldermanic railed enclosure and the Mayor took the chair. Among the members present was one lady who sat dumb in the rear (two other lady members were not present); the members were lawyers, doctors and representatives of both chambers. The Committee on Procedure presented their report (read by the clerk and not printed) which, instead of submitting standing orders and suggesting the order of business to be followed by the convention formulated three propositions as to the character of the charter; questions which they desired settled straight away by the convention that very evening.* It was round the first of these that the discussion raged. A stupid-looking young fellow,

---

* The following are the questions taken from the Report in the local newspaper:

" 'Your committee also reports that the convention express its opinion upon the following questions before the committees begin work, namely:

'First—Shall the executive powers of the city be divided as now between the mayor and the several boards, or shall there be one responsible executive head to the city government?

'Second—Shall amendments provide for home rule for Denver?

'Third—Shall an effort be made to submit the results of the labors of the convention to a vote of the people?' "

chairman of the Committee, insisted that the convention must choose between the present system whereby the Governor selected the principal administrators and the "one man System": what he exactly meant by this statement we failed to understand; the meeting assumed that the alternative was between the Governor and the Mayor as the "one-man." All the members of the convention were in favour of taking the power from the *Governor;* but there was a diversity of opinion as to whether it should be entrusted to the Mayor alone, or to the Mayor-in-Council, or to the electors. No one suggested that the resolution should be split into its component parts so that the voting should be on a clear issue. The Medical Officer of Health tried to suggest that Home Rule should be passed and that the more doubtful questions of the exact constitution of the Executive Authority should be left over for future discussion; and another member hinted that an Executive Board composed of elected officials and of the "Mayor in his Cabinet" might be a better alternative than one man power, pure and simple. No, the convention had made up its mind that there were only two alternatives— Appointment by the Governor of the State, and absolute power of the Mayor; so they voted for the resolution and practically settled the Charter before any enquiry or deliberation had been made. However, the convention was so muddle-headed that there is no reason why they should stick to their resolution.

The whole burden of the discussion was the evil of "divided responsibility." To-day the American has a perfect mania on this subject and it is extremely difficult for an Englishman to understand what he is aiming at. He is always taking about the necessity of making one man responsible. This usually consists in endowing one man with *irresponsible power*. He is placed in his position for a fixed period during which time he is irremovable and he is usually told that he will not be employed in any case again. It is therefore difficult to realise how exactly the American intends to control his autocrat or to make him "responsible" in any real sense. When we say that we hold a Cabinet or a Prime Minister *responsible* for the conduct of government we mean that we retain through our representatives our power of instant dismissal if their policy does not suit us. To hold a man responsible without power to punish him if he betrays his trust is sheer nonsense. All the Americans can hope for by this one-man power is to make the electors careful in their choice of the man to whom they give this *irresponsible* power. "Undivided responsibility" has become a catchword, in America, the meaning of which no-one quite understands but which when translated into the ordinary city charter turns out to be what we should call *irresponsible* power or autocracy.

We visited the genial little Governor again the next day at the Capitol. He took us to see the "Secretary of State" (elected by the people) an indifferent-looking clerk: two of the Judges of the Supreme Court who seemed sensible sort of persons, and generally he showed us around. In the course of conversation he volunteered the information that he had had to borrow the money from friends to pay the expenses of raising the Colorado companies for the war because there was no cash available for it in the State Treasury; also that Colorado was almost unable to pay the ordinary expense of Government owing to the fact that the constitution fixed the rate that could be raised on property and that as each county valued its own property the assessable value of the State was constantly going down! He was trying through the Supreme Court to get a decision whereby the State Government could exercise some real control over the operations of the County Assessors.

Sidney suggests that the analogy from American business organisation upon which the believers in One Man Power base their contention is false. If they mean that success follows upon One Man administering the business of which he is the principal partner or sole possessor, then they rely exclusively on the motive of self interest or responsibility to self. But this motive is absent in the Public Administrator who is not supposed to increase his own fortune or better his own position by the exercise of his public duties. If they mean the delegation by the Principal of his power over the several departments of his business to individual subordinates, then they forget that this delegation usually accompanied with continuance of office during good behavior, is coincident with power of instant dismissal should the subordinate fail to satisfy his Chief. When the history of American Railways comes to be written it will be interesting to see whether the disasters which have overtaken many of these enterprises in the past were not due to the irresponsible power of one man unchecked by any formal or informal Board of Directors; or whether the present stability of some of the present railways does not rest on the subordination of the chief executive official to groups of powerful shareholders who really direct the policy to be pursued.

It would be interesting to discover whether this childlike faith in the efficacy of one-man power is not a reaction from the theory of checks and balances introduced by the Federal Constitution. The principle with which the American statesmen started was that the one way to protect liberty was to break up power into little pieces and dole it out to different bodies of men or individual men, each one completely independent of each of the others, and all alike deriving their authority separately from the People. This theory was no doubt based on the fear of tyranny; of actual usurpation of power over the lives and property of individuals. Now no one fears tyranny: what a modern democracy requires is the conduct of its affairs with efficiency integrity and with due regard to the wishes of the whole community. This combination of efficiency with popular control is exactly what cannot be brought about by the theory of checks and balances. If each organ of government can be checked by another organ, if each individual administrator finds that his work can be nullified by another man or body of men, he inevitably loses heart in the straightforward performance of his duty and he feels moreover that under the circumstances he cannot be held *responsible* for what is done or left undone. And under this system there is no real guarantee that there will not be underground connivance of one man with another, of one body with another, in neglect of duty and in flagrant acts of dishonesty. No man or body of men stand out as supremely responsible for failure.

Rightly or wrongly we English think that supreme responsibility should be vested not in one man but in a body of men, and this for many reasons. In order to decide what course will meet with ultimate approval, it is well to have represented at the seat of Government, the main sections of the community itself. We need the deliberation of diverse minds and a large fund of common knowledge. Above all we must have *publicity*, which is or ought to be ensured by submitting questions to a deliberative assembly. We think, moreover, that it is more difficult to corrupt many men than one man; and far more difficult to do so secretly without it becoming generally known. But though we believe that this supreme power cannot be entrusted to one man we have never believed that government can be carried on *without* one supreme authority held responsible to the People. Thus we have endowed our Legislatures with control over administration as well as with the function of law making. There is no divided responsibility in the national or local governments of Great Britain. There is a chain of responsibilities. The Civil Service is responsible and therefore dependent on the Representatives, and the representative is dependent on the elector. The theory of checks and balances, of which the ordinary American is still so proud, is, in its worst sense, divided responsibility. It is the irony of fate that in order to escape the evils of this system in municipal government he is proposing to create an autocrat whose power shall be undivided irresponsible or secretly exercised. It is somewhat the same instinct which makes the American approve of the

usurpation of power and the secret and irresponsible exercise
of it by the Speaker of the House of Representatives, or still
worse, by the Boss of the Party Machine. The theory of
checks and balances, the refusal to construct one supremely
responsible body, leads inevitably either to subterranean
government by secret committees or to the creation of an
autocrat responsible to no-one during his tenure of office.

《*June 20th.*

A Sabbath week here regaining health. The bustle of the
great towns, the bad air and lack of exercise, the being entertained, expected to talk and tempted to eat, and finally an attack of the Chicago grippe, a villainous throat with fever, had
exhausted and enfeebled both of us. I had the special ail-
ment of neuralgia and toothache and I had developed a
mania of fear lest all my teeth were about to collapse, neces-
sitating difficult and disagreeable operations by incompetent
dentists. I was haunted by a vision of myself with at least
two of my front teeth, crowned some six years ago, absent
to all beholders besides suffering agonies of toothache unre-
lievable on the Pacific Ocean. So I arrived here a week ago
nerveless and dispirited, having become a prey to morbid
fears, constantly with me in the day-time and even recurring
in my dreams at night. But the high air and silent beauty of
this valley has strengthened my body and relieved my mind.
A Park-like stretch of pasture with fir-trees and granite
boulders grouped together in infinite variety of form and
shade, bounded on every side by rocky cliffs forming canyons
through which streams rush downward to merge in the Big
Thomson, a bright sparkling river running the length of the
valley. There is a peculiar charm in the colouring of the
pasture land. The basis is red granite gravel covered sparsely
with a soft blue-grey sweet-smelling herb with a silver shim-
mer in the sun; whilst wherever water flows a rich green reed
marks the borders. The same contrast in colouring between
the sad dark shaded pine which springs up on the higher

and drier ground and the luxuriant brilliancy of the young poplar which skirts in thick belts every flowing stream whether a little river or a mere rivulet. And rising up beyond the precipitous granite cliffs are the snow-clad peaks of the Rocky mountains which divide the Mississippi from the Pacific slope.

We spent our time lying at full length under the trees reading some dozen volumes of American History and Politics borrowed from the Denver municipal library we had brought with us: or wandering over the mountains. The last evening we talked with two Englishmen, Peters, the grandson of an old neighbour in Gloucestershire, (pleasant but worthless young fellow who had left England because he found "nothing to do there," sold his property and came away to wander about the world also doing nothing but doing it more pleasantly than he did in his own country) and a Captain Neville, a commonplace English aristocrat, not of much account, and with all the innate insolence of the irresponsible younger son. Otherwise we spoke to no-one and had a week's absolute rest from talk and enquiry.

《[*June 21st.*
We returned to Denver to the little Villa in which we lodged. The Biennial Convention of the Federated Women's Club consisting of some 1,000 delegates from all parts of the United States had taken possession of the little town and crowded into every available lodging. In one boarding house there were three ladies from Missouri, tall stiff women with furbelowed black silk skirts, dressy white bodices, and shoes, gloves, and odds and ends of jewelry all to match; hair elaborately frizzed, uninteresting expressions and formal but pleasant manners. "Dressiness" was indeed the characteristic note of the gathering. The theatre and churches at which the meetings were held were elaborately decorated with banners and flowers; the seats allotted to each state were betokened with gorgeous satin and silk banners, and the badges worn

by the delegates were light blue satin embroidered in gold. The crowd of women who filled the meetings would have been well-dressed if they had not been, according to English notions, over-dressed; there was a tiresome consciousness of artifice in the elaborately frilled "waists" and the cut about skirts. Low necks and jewel-bedecked hair were resorted to on the least excuse; and at the miscellaneous evening gatherings in Hotel parlours there was a display of diamonds of quite a competitive character. It was characteristic that we failed to get our credentials as speakers until the second afternoon because the Committee had insisted on having special badges printed for us! The meetings were never punctual, and the conduct of them was extremely amateurish. The lady who acted as Chairman would wander about the platform discussing procedure with one lady or another and standing up or sitting with little or no reference to whether she was addressing the meeting or listening to some one else. However, compared to gatherings of American men I do not know that it was as deficient in sense of procedure. Indeed seeing that there were no resolutions proposed, or discussions allowed, and that every member was "lady-like" there was little or no necessity for procedure of any sort. The papers read were not badly composed: they erred on the side of fine writing abounding in metaphors and grandiloquent phrases. There was a total absence of professional spirit or technical knowledge or even of practical intention. The best papers were by professional journalists and essay writers; who gave us elaborately prepared epigrams and clever and amusing anecdotes. Some of these speeches were admirably delivered with abundant gestures and "asides." The papers on social questions such as education etc., were mere résumés of the books the leading speakers had happened to read. I spoke one afternoon on "How to do away with the Sweating System" and though I was received with the usual courtesy and even enthusiasm, always shown to any English person who has any claim to distinction, I felt like a bull in a china shop. For the rest, these women were pleasant and lively, full of good intentions to improve their own minds, and with a sensitive and gracious deference to other persons' opinions, which makes all criticism seem mere ungraciousness.

It is difficult to estimate the worth of this "Club Movement." "Clubs" among American women are associations of the women in a given town who meet together periodically (either weekly or monthly) to read papers and talk. They usually devote themselves to literary subjects; but in the larger clubs they develop departments some of which aim at practical work: the establishment of kindergartens, domestic economy teaching for poorer women. They sometimes attempt civic reform or the promotion of some educative measure [in] the Legislature. But for the most part these clubs are simply mutual improvement societies; excuses for meetings at each others' houses, with something to talk about beyond servants and clothes. In constitution they differ enormously: some of them being very exclusive, others accepting any women who apply. The Eastern clubs tend to be limited; the Western unlimited, in their membership: but the dominant opinion is in favour of unlimited membership and against exclusiveness. One gathers that the Western clubs are more inclined for practical work than the clubs of New England and New York. At the present time there are said to be 600,-000 (?) Club women in the Federated Association: 35,000 in New York State alone, 1,000 in the Denver Club. We were told that the majority of the members of the Denver Club joined for social reasons as it was their only chance of gaining access to the "elegant" homes of the richer members. We have no analogous movement in England. When English women combine in associations it is always for some definite practical (usually political) purpose. But then the women who in England correspond to the majority of the Club women of America, do not join women's associations. "Society" without men seems to the English woman not worth having; and the exclusive spirit of English social life would prevent the upper class women from caring to associate with their middle and lower middle class sisters unless impelled by a political motive, or reforming impulse of some kind or another. The Club Movement in America represents only the more intellectual, and little more than a desire on their part for a smattering of culture without effort. On the practical side, it embodies good intention towards social reform without the requisite knowledge. But it does exhibit a genuine desire in the American women of all classes for social equality and a graciousness and kindliness of disposition which is usually absent among our own women. To the women in the little towns and villages scattered over the vast plains of America, the Club Movement means the yearning for a wider life and brings to them a feeling of fellowship with other women, which may be the beginning of a desire for active citizenship. And in criticising the segregation of the women apart from the men, an Englishwoman is apt to forget that American women find that their husbands, fathers and brothers have little or no public interests and are not characterised by intellectual curiosity; and that they are therefore to a large extent thrown on each other for any kind of stimulus to self-improvement or public work.

Complete adult women's suffrage has now been in force for four years in Colorado. There is a universal consensus of opinion that as far as the women's vote has had any distinctive influence at all, it has been an influence for good. The women have in the main voted with their husbands and masters, but a certain section of advanced women have influenced the votes of both sexes in favour of good government. And the women's vote has ousted certain evil livers and corrupt politicians from the State and Municipal Government, and has made the successful candidates more circumspect in their behaviour. Otherwise the women do not seem to have brought more wisdom into politics; they have only black-balled open corruption. There are three women in the House of Representatives who have not as yet distinguished themselves. They are said to come of much the same class as the male representatives. The State Superintendent of Education is a woman, and many of the country superintendants. It is indeed in educational matters that the woman's vote takes the keenest interest, and here she is said to vote for candidates who have "progressive" ideas. At all other elections, if she shows any independant judgment, she votes for what she imagines to be the "good man" whatever may be his opinions or policy. Mrs. Dickinson and other intelligent women who had been enthusiastic for women's suffrage are now somewhat pessimistic: they say that the women officials are not more competent or less open to corruption that the men, and that the ward politician type is appearing among the women who take active part in politics. On the other hand, most of the former opponents to women's suffrage admit that it has produced absolutely no change in the woman at home and no appreciable change in political life except the exclusion of the most vicious representatives. The Conservative who objects to universal suffrage naturally enough objects to its extension to women, as it increases the disproportion between the non-propertied and propertied electors. On the whole, judged merely by results on government, I am inclined to believe women's suffrage in America has been justified. The women—especially the women of leisure have better intentions than the men, and they are not more politically incapable. They have also a greater desire for information.

¶[*Leadville*. Mining camp of 15,000 population; has been 30 or 40,000. Incorporated as city of second class in 1899 [in fact, 1878]. Formerly had twelve Aldermen, two from each of six districts: reduced number to six as "more conducive to conduct of business." Mayor acts as chairman and nominates Committees which have to be approved by Board of Aldermen. He has no veto, and is elected by popular vote for two years. (So also City Treasurer, City Attorney and Marshall Head of police). The elected officials (not the Mayor) are removable by Board (on cause shown) who can fill up the post vacant pending the next election. All other offices filled by Board. The Mayor is chairman of Board of Health. Also he nominates two Aldermen and one citizen who, with the Medical Officer of Health, makes the Board of Health. The first municipal government was very corrupt and parted with water and gas franchise on improvident terms and left the city saddled with debt of £200,000. As a reaction a Populist Government which though not corrupt, was inefficient, and became, according to the present Mayor, discredited by non-fulfilment of demogagic promises. After the great strike with riots and disorder the citizens elected a respectable conservative set of men who were apparently conducting the affairs with humdrum economy. Present Mayor was a mine managers' candidate, himself being a manager. The city revenue consists of a limited rate (2%) on assessed values, (value assessed by elected county official who fixes it at half the value of the property?) and of proceeds from licences.

The Mayor [Charles E. Dickinson] came to see us: a slow-speaking quiet individual—not a politician. He was elected by the largest majority ever polled for Mayor in Leadville; a reaction from the Populist Government. We gather that it is the miners' organisations which were the backbone of the populists wave in Colorado. Just before the great strike of eight months they had got hold of every office in the city and county from the Mayor and Aldermen to the District Judge and County Sheriff. For some time there was anarchy in Leadville; the authorities refusing to keep order and the mine-managers arming volunteers with the newest rifles. After one or two mines had been blown up by the strikers and some strikers shot by the volunteers, the Governor of the State (the one who *succeeded* [Davis H. "Bloody Bridles"] Waite the Populist) sent in one thousand State militia who remained here for months. The strike collapsed and the Populist party was defeated at the next city election. (In the State they had already lost control.) Altogether one gathers that the Populist party is at present shrinking up in Colorado as elsewhere.

Leadville is a desolate place. It stands ten thousand feet above the sea; the mountains rise abruptly from the plateau on all sides in finely moulded forms. Thus there is an element of grandeur in its situation. But for miles around the plain is one vast grave ground of fir trees: its sandy space dotted over with old stumps mostly charred; mere remnants left over from the zealous destruction of the charcoal burner aided by the forest fires. The arid waste of the mountainsides and peaks seemed like sections of desert raised on high by some subterranean force; the glaring sunlight showing up the absolute barrenness of their parched surfaces. The shafts of the mines, the black smoke of the blasting furnaces, the squalid rows of one-storied wooden huts which make up the city, the clouds of dust, which sweep through the streets, the alternate blazing sun and bitter wind, all add to its desolateness. Nor does the social life seem particularly inspiring. In the old days of a new mining camp, with 30,000 inhabitants, Leadville was the scene of desperate adventures and the abiding place of desperate characters. Now that its mineral resources are definitely known and definitely owned, the floating population of speculators, card-sharpers and bullies has left for "greener" ground, and the inhabitants have settled down to a dull routine of money-getting. When not working there is no recreation for the clerk, or the working-man, but the billiard table and a mild kind of gambling. At the rambling, dirty Hotel at which we stayed there was always a body of middle class men, lounging or smoking by the log fire in the Hall. As we sauntered down the streets on Saturday evening, the saloons were full to overflowing (though it is fair to add we saw no man worse for drink). The barber shops were crowded, and at each corner of the street there were knots of bored citizens. Throughout this community the spirit of restlessness wrestles with a spirit of bored apathy; the present desire "to move on" checked by indecision as to where to go to! And from all accounts that is their attitude as electors and citizens: the bulk of the population ready to take up with any new idea that comes along and to discard it with equal facility:—a period of indifference being followed by another wave of political excitement over some new shibboleth. Not promising material for a reform movement.

([*June 29th, Utah Salt Lake City.*

I remember the Salt Lake City of twenty-five years ago as a town of wooden cottages surrounded by gardens with streams of mountain water running on each side of the way, every garden taking its lot.* Now it has great stone and brick buildings, tram lines and telegraph wires; and the streams of water which I remember have disappeared below the pavement of the dirty streets. Viewed from the tower of the new county hall building it has still the look of a garden of trees and green turf, with houses planted in their midst. But the garden, instead of being bounded sharply by a parched desert, now fades away imperceptibly into cultivated farms far away into the distance to the foot of the parched and rocky mountains. As we steamed through the plain I was struck with the fine fair buildings, the orchards of fruit-trees, the acres of well cultivated wheat, potatoes and roots of all kinds. Utah plain is perhaps the most highly cultivated land we have seen in America; far more diversified in its culture than the rolling plains of Illinois.

The city and county hall is a fine building, somewhat overpretentious in its architecture, but inside admirably adapted to its purpose. And it is beautifully clean and well-kept, the first really *self-respecting* abode of a municipal authority we have come across in the United States. By acci-

---

* I visited Utah in 1873 as a girl of fifteen with Arthur Playne and sister Kate, during a trip to San Francisco, when father was President of the Grand Trunk Railway of Canada.

dent or habit there were no loungers, neither in the afternoon
when we went to find the mayor, nor in the evening when
we returned to attend the city council. The council chamber
was a model of comfort and simple tastefulness of decoration;
and on the tables of the president, the recorder and the reporters, there were bouquets of bright flowers. During the
session there was neither smoking nor spitting. The fifteen
members were a decent looking lot; better dressed and more
quietly behaved than any other council we have yet visited.
There was very little talking and the members appeared
really attending to the business in hand. The same procedure
as in other American municipalities but far more decorum
in carrying it out. The reports of committees were passed
rapidly or debated with good temper and competence. No
sign of the ward politician. Remarkably little yankee twang.
The mayor [John Clark] sat at a table in the corner: a stolid
respectable middle-class man who evidently had his friends
among the council who would come and consult with him
and then get up and speak as if he were not present. When
we presented our introduction he took us into his inner office
(charmingly fitted up, with a big posy of flowers on the writing table) and with a good deal of reserve and slowness of
speech answered our questions. From him and others we
gathered the following facts as to the municipal history of
Salt Lake City.

Incorporated 1860 and governed until 1890 by Mormons,
parsimoniously but without corruption. In 1891 an anti-
Mormon or liberal administration came into power: the
mayor said they squandered the rate-payers' money; the city
Recorder (like the Mayor a Mormon) thought that the lib-
erals had "made the city": they had paved the streets, carried
out a sewage system, built the City Hall and altogether
changed Salt Lake City from a village to a city. But apparently at the end of their reign corruption had set in and
boodling was rife. Meanwhile the cleavage in political parties
had altered from Mormon and Liberal to Republican and

Democrats. Moreover the propertied classes had taken fright at the expenditure of the Liberal administration. The City had been run into debt exceeding the legal limit, but the rates were still only equal to two months rent. Over and above the two parties a "non-partisan party" appeared in the field headed by Clark (present Mayor, and Mormon) and the editor of the Gentile organ (the *Tribune*). On both the two political party tickets Mormons appeared, the Democratic list being almost exclusively composed of "Saints." The victory would have been overwhelmingly Democratic if the non-partisan ticket had not split the vote. The council returned last autumn was composed of eleven Democrats, two non-partisans, two Republicans; or taken on the religious cleavage, thirteen Mormons, two Gentiles (two Republicans) and a non-partisan Mayor and Auditor (Mormon); the City Recorder, Treasurer, and Attorney being Democrats and Mormons. The calibre of the Council is said to be higher than it has been for many years, well-to-do citizens coming forward as candidates for all parties. The Mayor is himself a wealthy business man (wholesale ironmonger and grocer).

We gathered there had been frequent changes in the Charter: originally the Mayor presided over the Council and had no veto. That was altered in 1892 to the American plan of complete separation between legislature and executive, except that the Mayor can veto any law unless Council persists in passing it by two-thirds vote. It was said that when the Mayor and Council disagreed on some question of appointment, the Mayor became too angry to be a good president.* The President of the Council selects the Committees of the Council which seem to be living bodies. A Police and Fire Board had been created by the State Legislature (appointed two by the Mayor and two by the Council), but had been recently disestablished and the Mayor and Council reign supreme. The Mayor claims to have sole power of *nomina-*

* I can well understand that an independently elected Mayor with co-ordinated authority with the Council would be an unfit "Speaker."

tion of all Executive officials; (I gather that the city recorder thinks that is not so) the council having simply a veto on appointments. There is a Board of Public Works, which seems to be on the point of disestablishment, partly because it is Republican and partly because the Council considers that public works have come to an end and the salaried Board is unnecessary. All executive officers are changed with change of administration except perhaps some of the firemen and policemen.

We revisited the County Hall the next morning with a note to the janitor, a delightful old man—native of Durham and early convert to Mormonism, who had pushed his hand cart across the desert in search of the city of Zion. He had that shrewd and pious nature that one associates with north country miners. We now understood why the County and City Hall was unlike any other American municipal abode, and the fact that besides being janitor he was a member of the municipal council and chairman of the parks committee explained the profusion of flowers. He showed us over the building and took us to the Tower, talking all of while of the council, the mayor, the governor, and in a reserved and rather shy way, of Mormonism itself. With him we went into the County Recorders' office—in which are filed the titles to land, mortgages and transfers. This office was opened by Brigham Young in the first years of the settlement, and in its perfectly kept books you can trace the ownership and circumstance of every rood of land. B. Young tried to instil into his people the doctrine of usufruct, e.g.—that no man should possess more land than he could cultivate. But with the intrusion of gentiles with money to spare, came the mortgage, and with the mortgage the gradual accumulation of land in the hands of a few persons who held it as an investment. But even at the present time the occupier is usually the owner.

Governor Wills [Heber M. Wells], to whom Governor Adams of Colorado had given us an introduction, we found at the state bank of which he is cashier (manager). The son of Squire Wills, a rich Mormon, he belongs to the Mormon aristocracy and had evidently been "put up" by the Republicans to catch the Mormon vote, or had turned Republican to catch the Republican vote. He looked an able straight forward, not distinguished, young man, a wholesome fellow, more the church member than the politician. Like the mayor and the janitor, he was reserved about the Church, though anxious we should meet some of their "leading" members. When one reads the miserable plagiarisms of the Book of Mormon and the second-rate occultism of most of their religious tracts one marvels why such cautious and level-headed individuals as the elderly mayor or the young governor should abide by the doctrines and discipline of this strange sect. The Governor endowed us richly with volumes of the city and state ordinances, and reports of the sessions of the legislature. About the results of woman suffrage his tone was uncertain: the women in the senate and house of representatives had not, he said, accomplished anything except a law prohibiting large hats at places of amusement—a law, he added, which had been carried "out of courtesy" by the men. The suffrage had been granted to the women by the Mormon territorial legislature of Utah in 1890, it had been taken from them by a federal act in 1886, both measures being passed because in one case the change increased, and in the other diminished, the Mormon majority in the state. In good old times the women had only voted, they had not aspired to office. Now the spirit had changed: one Mormon lady actually running against her husband and beating him for a state senatorship. Our curiosity with regard to this lady was naturally aroused—specially as the Governor added that the lady Senator—Mrs. Cannan—was one of the several wives of an influential elder of the church. Was this a revolted wife who was using her political rights to punish her husband for past enjoyment of his religious rights to many wives? Or was she among those whom the Mormon chief had been forced to relinquish by the United States law? When therefore the jovial Mormon city recorder suggested that we should see Mrs. Cannan and offered an introduction, we forthwith accepted.

A little wooden villa, overshadowed by trees and in the neighbourhood of the Temple, was marked out as her abode by a notice board attached to the wicket gate. *Dr. Hughes: Office Hours two to four,* for we had been told that she practised medicine under that name. It was already past these office hours, there was no sign that the house was inhabited. So I tucked my card and letter of introduction under the door and gave up the hope of seeing her. But the next morning, the day of our departure, after seeing over the Tabernacle, we had time to spare and wandered round to her house on the chance that we might catch her. Just in front of us, as we stood at the wicket gate, were two women—a poor woman in a blue blouse and skirt, and a sprightly pleasant-looking little person with energetic gait and decided manner —obviously our senator, medical practitioner and plural wife. We followed them into the little consulting room and I introduced myself. "Delighted to see you Mrs. Webb: I had been meaning this morning to call on you: excuse me a moment: this is a lady patient of mine." In a few minutes she was back again and we opened our questions, keeping strictly to woman suffrage: "How had the woman representatives succeeded in the legislature?" For the first half hour she was on her guard: she had little to say about women's suffrage except that she was enthusiastically in favour of it. We were sympathetic and took every occasion to refer respectfully to "the Church" as it was clear she was a pious Mormon. We asked whether it was true that the women in the late election had run behind their ticket. That suggestion roused her "I suppose your informant referred to me: but mine was an exceptional case. Of course I do not want this to be reported" she said, gaining confidence in us, "but I would like you to know the truth" she added with a certain sensitive frankness. "There have been so many false reports spread through the

Press." And then followed the whole story. She was one of Mr. Cannan's wives and had been asked by the Democratic party to stand for a senatorship long before there was any idea that her husband would be nominated by the Republicans. But besides herself the Democrats had put forward a noted Mormon elder—Caine by name. Then the Republicans, in order to gain the Mormon vote, had persuaded Mr. Cannan and Mrs. Emmeline Wells (one of Squire Wells' widows) to come forward, each party running also one gentile to make up a full ticket for the division. It was represented that she was running against her husband: as a matter of fact she ran against Mrs. Wells. Meanwhile the Church issued instructions that the faithful were to vote for Caine, Cannan & Wells leaving her off the list because, as she asserted "they wanted Brother Cannan; they had no spite against me, but naturally enough they did not want two of a family. And Mr. Cannan was not a bit hurt at my standing: he met me the day before the poll and said 'now how do you expect to come out my girl;' I really believe he wished me to win. As it turned out the great Democratic wave carried the whole party list; but as some Mormon Democrats did not vote for me because they voted for my husband, and some gentiles did not vote for me because I was a 'plural wife' I actually came out the lowest successful candidate for the district."

By this time we had made it clear that we had no foolish prejudices against the tenets of the Mormon creed, and I ventured boldly with the question: "Do you think plural marriages are an advantage or a disadvantage to the Mormon Church?" "An advantage undoubtedly" the little woman answered. Then followed her whole theory of polygamy. The Church had believed in it for mystic reasons: they held that innumerable spirits were seeking re-incarnation and that it was a duty laid upon the Saints to provide for this re-incarnation in pious households by each Saint taking unto himself as many wives as he could fairly support and protect. Each

Mormon was the inspired priest and patriarch of a family, the more numerous the family the greater his honour. But this, she signified, was the church's view, she was content to let polygamy be judged on more practical grounds. It was an enormous advantage, she asserted for a woman to be able to select a really good man as father to her children instead of putting up with any miserable fellow who might be left over by other women. The finest men could have almost unlimited children providing they were allowed unlimited wives; and their stock was wasted if they were forced to limit their reproduction to the capacity of one woman. Moreover, a woman might be satisfied with one or two children and seldom needed more in a husband than a kind protector: her children satisfied her instincts. Sometimes she would like to follow a profession, any way she did not want to be always bearing children. Then Mrs. Cannan delicately but frankly intimated the existence of a "celestial law" unwritten but privately taught to the men, whereby it was unlawful for a husband to claim his rights during pregnancy or lactation. This law could not be fulfilled without polygamy or prostitution: prostitution was the source of disease, polygamy of healthy procreation. "Of course," she continued, "it is said that there were jealousies and pettiness among the wives: that may be so; it would be surprising if women bred up with monogamous traditions were to adapt themselves to the higher and purer feeling. The truth is," she added, "the experiment was not tried long enough to judge by results: when Mormons point to the beautiful healthy children born in the homes of our Saints I sometimes suggest that we owe something to outdoor life in a splendid climate. But I believe that polygamy is based on fundamental truths, physiological and psychological; and that if the law had been honestly practised according to the doctrine of the church and maintained by the law of the State, then we should have become a splendid race and converted the world to our creed."

"Do you think, Mrs. Cannan, that polygamy favours the

independence of women?" "Well, honestly I can't say it has done so: the women believed that their husbands were priests as well as husbands. Whatever John said was law. But it *would* in time, have worked out to independence" said the little woman undaunted. "It gave the woman more real physical freedom: if they chose, they could have had an independent life; they were not completely absorbed as one wife is in her husband. I wish you were staying longer: I should like you to see Mrs. Amelia Young: I should like to take you to see Mr. Cannan: he is a splendid man: he would give you a much better vision of the Mormon creed than I can."

From polygamy the conversation drifted to the Mormon creed. Mrs. Cannan was one of those typical American women who have picked up some of the generalisations and a good deal of the phraseology of modern science without any understanding of its methods—with no conception for instance, that there exists such a process as *verification*. She was an occultist and therefore believed that to-day there was constant communication with spirits; she was a believer in authority as a necessary part of faith in a church: therefore the head of the church had constant communication with the eternal Father. It was clear from the little glimpses she gave us, that in organisation the Mormon church rested on the same principle of hierarchical authority as the Catholic church. As Sidney remarked, all the men who, from their position in the church were possible future presidents, are elderly if not aged men. Brigham Young, when he lead the Mormons into the wilderness and built up Utah State was a man in the prime of life. Today the Mormon policy is shrewd but it is over-cautious—a caution which is levelling its tenets and discipline down to the standard of an ordinary Evangical Christian sect.

We left our vivacious frank little Senator with regret; she was such a self-respectful vigourous pure-minded little soul: sensitive yet unself-conscious, indiscreet yet loyal. She had no training for the political career she had chosen, and I suspect her medical knowledge was as fragmentary as her economics. As a citizen I should doubt her wisdom as a legislator—and as a patient I certainly should not trust her skill in diagnosing my case. But as a friend I should rely on her warm sympathy and freedom from the meaner motives of life.

As for her arguments in favour of polygamy, they obviously went further than the institution. "Scientific breeding" can hardly be confined to the selection of the man. Polygamy, however, takes into account the enormously disproportionate prolificness of the male, and therefore the possibility of a much higher degree of selection than in the case of the female. Only one bull is required for twenty cows. As a social arrangement it has also a justification: many women are satisfied with children and are bored and over-worked if they also have to serve as wife-companion to the father of those children. It is the childless woman who makes the best wife to the professional man! As for the religious side of the institution, it is based on an old truth—that woman's sexual feeling towards the man is, in many cases, indistinguishable from her reverence towards and obedience to the Priest; religious sentiment being very closely related to sexual instincts. But this old truth is one of those facts which we want to abolish by ignoring it, not to strengthen by stereotyping it into an institution. For the rest, I agree with Mrs. Cannan, that it is a loss to the world that the experiment of polygamy was not continued by a sect exceptionally well-fitted to give it a fair and full trial and to develop the experiment into other forms of "scientific breeding" if polygamy pure and simple proved unsatisfactory.

Among other Mormon experiments was the great Zion Mercantile Cooperative Institution, established by B. Young to provide commodities for the Saints at cost price. Unfortunately he did not know of the Rochdale plan, and gave the profits and control to members as capitalists. The institution has therefore inevitably drifted into an ordinary Capitalist corporation, the capital and control becoming more and more largely held by Eastern stockholders and corporations. It will soon cease to be a Mormon institution, and will be one among many Departmental Stores in Salt Lake City.*

As we steamed out of Salt Lake City we felt aggravated that we had only left two days, since we had openings to see a good deal more of Mormon Society than we had expected.

([*San Francisco. July 2nd to 7th.*

We brought introductions from Michael Davitt to the editor of the *Star*—a weekly Irish paper. The result was an invitation to ride in the July 4th procession from the Irish chairman of the celebration committee which for some reason or another seemed made up of Irish politicians. For two days and nights existence was made hideous by the firing off of crackers and pistols by all the youths of San Francisco, the noise becoming acute towards midnight, and lasting without cessation until the morning of the 5th. There was something strange about the imperturbable way in which the whole youthful population turned out into the streets and betook itself to this occupation of firing, as if it were some religious rite that had to be performed, no laughter, no talking, simply bang, bang, bang, straight at the pavements so as to create the maximum sound, the grim silence of the actors contrasting with the deafening results of their action. Whether the youthful San Franciscan felt himself to be firing at the Spaniards, or whether he has caught the Chinese love of mere mechanical noise, I cannot tell; but, to the Englishman accustomed to the subdued sounds of the most crowded London streets, this quick succession of explosions was an excruciating addition to the wanton rattle and roar of the American street. Certainly our last impression of an American city will be like our first of New York: Noise, noise, noth-

---

* Sidney remarks that this is not correct: the institution, whatever may be its future, is at present in the hands of the Mormons.

ing but noise. That is the curse both of American city life and of American travelling. In the city your senses are disturbed, your ears are deafened, your eyes are wearied by a constant rush; your nerves and muscles are shaken and rattled in the street cars; you are never left for one minute alone on the road, whether you travel by ordinary car or Pullman; doors are opened and slammed, passengers jump up and down, boys with papers, sweets, fruits, drinks, stream in and out and insist on your looking at their wares or force you to repel them rudely; conductors shut and open windows; light and put out the gas; the engine bell rings constantly, and now and again the steam whistle (more like a fog-horn than a whistle) thunders out warning of the train's approach. Noise, confusion, rattle and bustle are among the disagreeable memories of American travel.

But the procession. The committee of Irish politicians met at our hotel and when we came down were standing about the hall: they were ornamented with grand ribbons and gold and silver trappings, or bustling about the carriages already decked with plentiful drapings of stars and stripes. We were ushered into a carriage with Chief Justice Beattie [William Henry Beatty] (California State Supreme Court) a shrewd and kindly old gentleman of Scotch descent and southern breeding. The editor of the Star—an Irishman with an unhealthy look and blatant talk—completed the party. Trevelyan, who had arrived from Portland that morning, was put in a carriage with the two police magistrates, fat, big Irishmen who escaped from the carriage to drink at saloons in the long waits and were received with cheers from all the other saloons on the way. We had an agreeable morning, for our Chief Justice discussed with acumen American law—the relation of federal and state courts, and entertained us with bar stories. He was a dignified person, said to be upright and honourable even by his opponents, somewhat cynical with regard to the American constitution, but kindly and fair in his tone. He thought "government by injunction" had been

carried too far by some of the inferior courts: but approved
of the principle: asserted that it was the only way in which
acts which were not illegal but were injurious could be prevented. A dangerous admission to make to the opponents of
injunctions! The procession did not come to much: the mar-
shalling was amateurish, the troops were raw, with a mini-
mum of uniform and drill. But these American youths as they
filed past us had the charm of a high standard of manners
and intelligence—not rowdiness; might have been Sunday
school teachers or ambitious young journeymen anxious to
marry their masters' daughters: (as a matter of fact I believe
they are mostly sons of well-to-do parents).

In the afternoon we attended the "literary exercises" in a
crowded hall. These consisted of a plentiful supply of bad
music, choruses, solos and orchestral overtures, all alike being refrains and varieties of the Star Spangled Banner: a welcoming speech from the Irish mayor and an oration from an
Irish orator, a glowing tribute to the "Liberty, Independence
and Free Institutions" of America. The celebration con-
cluded with a recitation of the *Declaration of Independence*
by some well-known elocutionist. The note of the whole
thing was the unique character of American Institutions—
the "only Democracy of the World"—the Americans being
the chosen people who had, by their own greatness of soul,
discovered freedom, and who were now to carry it to other
races (notably to the Cubans). The *Declaration of Independence* was received with deafening applause as if this
declaration had been made yesterday and sealed by the
blood of the present generation. "That all men are born free
and equal," was announced as a bran new revelation from
heaven and received by the audience as if it were the basis
of their existence. Altogether the thought that this sort of
stuff was being repeated in every city and village in the
United States made one realise how French is American
patriotic sentiment: how anxious to assure itself of the

nation's glory and how swaddled up in abstract propositions which have long since lost their meaning.

The following day we spent with San Francisco's municipal institutions. At the present time it is governed by some half dozen authorities. There is a Board of Supervisors, twelve in number, elected by the inhabitants of San Francisco itself; but on the queerest of electoral methods. We have often noted the disadvantage of the American law or custom of forcing a man to live in his electoral district—this residential qualification playing into the hands of the ward politician and depriving the poorer districts of the chance of selecting able men of standing as representatives. The constitution-makers of San Francisco seem to have had some sort of suspicion of the fact: but instead of doing away with the residential qualification they have done away with electoral districts! Today each supervisor has to live in the district he "represents" but he is elected by the whole of San Francisco to represent that district! This Board of Supervision has always been one of the most corrupt among American Councils: the two years term of a Supervisor is reckoned to "bring in" $40,000. As these supervisors fix the rate to be charged by the Water Company their "price" is secured virtually by statute. The Mayor has little power as the Police, Fire, Harbour and Park Boards are appointed by the Governor; *but he presides over the Board of Supervisors* and appoints some of the members of the Board of Elections. The Superintendent of Streets, who does most of the public work, is elected; so also, I presume, the Comptroller, Auditor and City Attorney. There is a Board of Education separately elected at large. This constitution dates from 1855 but has been amended almost every year by the State Legislature. San Francisco however, like all other American cities, is discontented with its existing form of government and has recently carried by referendum a new constitution, giving the Mayor the whole appointing power and "checking" the action of the Board of Supervisors by the Mayor's veto, and a referendum of all grants of franchises direct to the people. This constitution was drafted by a Committee of a hundred appointed by the present Mayor, the draft being submitted to a committee of fifteen elected by the people and then ratified by the people themselves. It awaits the approval of the State Legislature.

The Mayor [James D. Phelan] is a decent little fellow: one of the wealthiest of San Francisco's citizens, an Irishman by extraction whose father was fortunate enough to speculate in the right acre of ground and to have his title approved of by the courts. The great Phelan is a dapper little person; ambitious and public-spirited, but without any special distinction of body or soul. He entertained us at a sumptuous lunch in a private room at a restaurant at which the one "Honorable Supervisor," a refined and gentle-natured medical practitioner, and the inevitable Irish Editor were present. He told us of a *coup d'etat* he had attempted. By a provision of the constitution the supervisors are obliged to fix the water rate before a certain date: last year they failed to do so, so the Mayor, who had been waiting to get rid of the corrupt body, applied to a city court who obligingly declared their seats vacant, whereupon the Mayor appointed twelve upright men. The elected representatives of the people stuck to their seats, lived night and day in the Board room, and had to be finally ejected by the police. But they returned in triumph: the State Supreme Court overriding the inferior Court's decision and re-instating them. It is characteristic of the good-nature of American political life that the Mayor still presides quite amicably over the Supervisors whom he ejected by the police, and who, a few weeks later, ejected his nominees by order of the Supreme Court!

We heard a good deal of vague abuse of the constitution of California, and from undemocratic friends still more of the interpretation of it by the State Supreme Court. On the other hand the Chief Justice and his colleagues of the Supreme

Court were chuckling over the fact that most of its absurd provisions had been incapable of interpretation, whilst others had enabled them to declare half the laws passed by the Legislature "unconstitutional." These shrewd, old men (whom we were invited to meet at the Chief Justice's chambers) seemed to be the rulers of California. They were against the anti-capitalist provisions of the constitution and determined to make what they considered "common sense" out of the tangle of demagogic statutes. The Irish Editor hinted that all but Beattie were bought: but it was easy to see that the constitutional bias of their commonplace but hard headed minds was against the sort of ideas thrown up by the chaotic democracy of California.

San Francisco seems to belong neither to the East nor to the West. There is none of that extreme sensitiveness of Eastern opinion that one notices in cities west of Chicago; neither is there any desire nor effort to declare its independence of the East. It seems isolated from and unconcerned with any other part of America. It is out and away the most cosmopolitan city I have yet come across. It has no standards, no common customs; no common ideals of excellence, of intellect or manners—only one universal anarchy, each race living according to its own lights, or rather according to its own impulses, seeing that all alike are free from their own racial public opinion. To the person who wishes to live unto himself without any pressure of law, custom or public opinion, San Francisco must be a Haven. If he combines with this "individualism" a Bohemian liking for variety of costume, manners, morals and opinions, San Francisco must be a veritable paradise. So thought the burley Scotch merchant —a confirmed old bachelor who entertained us at dinner the last night of our stay in the United States. "I would na go back to Great Britain for a fortune. I sometimes have a passing wish for a moor with a blinding Scotch mist sweeping over me; but the shackled life of Glasgow, Edinburgh or London—I could na return to it."

《[*On Board the Coptic, July 10th.*

General Impressions of America. We cannot pretend to have studied America or the Americans. We have focussed our attention on Municipal Government, but even here our enquiry has been superficial. We have interviewed individuals and observed the working of the machine, but our information has been for the most part unverified and some of the details given in our notes are certain to be incorrect. I would, therefore, warn any future reader of my diary not to take my statements as authoritative. I have done my best to retail accurately what I have seen and heard, but I have seldom been able to verify the information by other testimony or by further observation, or by reference to documents. Still, as a general impression of the structure and working of American municipal government I think my notes must have some validity, as it is unlikely that we have in all the cases been deceived. It seems now worth while to gather together our general impression of the people and their political life into a generalised form.

SUPERFICIAL NOTES ON AMERICAN CHARACTERISTICS
JULY 1898

Who would recognise as distinctively American the essentially eccentric and ugly individuals portrayed by Dickens, Trollope and Martineau? All the peculiar characteristics of the American of that time seem to be reversed in the American of to-day. Take, for instance, the bad manners attributed to the American by the English travellers of the first half of the nineteenth century. Of all the white races the Americans have to-day the most agreeable manners: they are most adept in social amenities. Whether you visit the club or the drawing room of good society, or hold on by the strap in a crowded street car, you never feel snubbed or ignored. You never watch ugly or weak people intentionally pained in body or mind; you seldom or ever hear an insolent word or a low jest. There is not only an absence of brutality and coarseness, there is a positive presence of kindliness and humanity—an atmosphere of hospitality towards all sorts and conditions of men, a contagious desire that all alike should have a good time. And this dominant good temper is transformed into good manners by an absence of all we English call snobbishness. A typical American—and the further west you go the more typical he becomes in this respect—never asks "who you are" or otherwise takes your measure before he begins to be civil. In their everyday intercourse, citizens of the United States have to a large extent "chosen equality" and with this choice they have acquired the most essential part of good breeding.

In a yet deeper sense the Americans are well-mannered. The native-born citizen has his physical instincts well under control. He eats and drinks moderately; he respects womanhood, and chastity is the rule and not the exception. One of the pleasantest impressions of our visit to the U.S.A. is the clear eye and modest expression of the American youth, whether you see him at the University, in the office, or in the recruiting camp. Even if you meet him rollicking with his comrades in the street or the cars, he seldom shows raw animalism in act or gesture. It is indeed one of the surprises of this continent that under the influence of American customs and traditions, the heterogeneous population of a mining camp or the ungoverned inhabitants of a frontier town, rapidly settle down to the orderly ways and clean habits typical of American civilisation. And these good manners do not mean effeminacy. No race excels the American in physical courage. If nervous will-power and sheer delight in using it, if love of risks—at any rate physical and financial risks, are the test of virility, the American has no peer.

It is difficult to be as enthusiastic over any other American characteristic. All their other qualities seem to be counterbalanced by defects, to be, in fact, the other side of these defects. Take for instance their extraordinary promptness

in making decisions; the marvellous rapidity with which all
their faculties respond to their will and result in action. With
the American there is no time lost between the intention and
the act. "No sooner said than done" might be taken as one
of the national mottos. Indeed, if the affairs of life were
nothing more than a series of emergencies, arising acciden-
tally and without the possibility of pre-knowledge—emergencies which had necessarily to be met by action without
time for consideration, I doubt whether any other race could
compete successfully with the American. But this capacity
for prompt and unhesitating decision is the other side of
their gravest national defect—impatience. No result is worth
waiting for; no idea is worth testing; no achievement is worth
a life time; no man, no machine, no system, no Government,
is worth keeping if some new man, machine, system or government promises immediate betterment. And one may add,
no reform is worth persistently fighting for unless it can be
immediately obtained. To this inability to think out things
and to persist is due that strangest of paradoxes of American
political life, its continuous restlessness and its relative stag-
nation. Social changes are always being threatened, but they
are seldom attained. A new scheme of reform is put forward,
is accepted, yields its crop of extravagant hopes and extravagant fears and then dies down long before it has taken a
practical shape. One wonders whether it is a consciousness
of this unstable political equilibrium, combined with incapacity to think things out, that makes the American statesman tolerate so complacently and even advocate enthusiastically the bondage to a written constitution which can
with difficulty be changed.

One incidental result of this same impatience is the delight
of the American in time-saving contrivances, combined with
an apparent contempt for the value of time. If perfectly con-
structed telephones, skilled stenographers, express elevators,
electric signals of all description, could by themselves get
through business, the transactions of one American city

would exceed those of the world. But as far as we could make out, the very ease and rapidity with which every individual business man can gratify his impulse to get into communication with every other business man and insist on being attended to there and then, ends in a general dissipation of energy and such destruction of continuity of effort that fewer transactions were actually completed than would have been the case if each man had been compelled to get through his work without immediately consulting other people. All this appreciation of mechanical contrivances seems to us a symptom of the American's disinclination to think beforehand or to do things or permit other people to do things in any methodical sequence. Each individual business man becomes the slave of all the stray impulses and sudden improvisations of all other business men. No man—not even the biggest Boss, has any considerable time left him for consecutive thinking. From our observations of Americans engaged in law, in business and in public life, I very much doubt whether, with all the perfection of mechanical devices, with far longer hours in the year devoted to work and with a much greater expenditure of nervous force, the American man of affairs actually gets through more or even as much solid work as the leisure loving Englishman or the methodically industrious German.

To settle whether the Americans are among the deliberate or the impulsive races is therefore a puzzle. If a high degree of control over physical organs and mental faculties is the test, then the Americans are the least impulsive of human beings. If long-sighted and persistently pursued action, based on carefully ascertained knowledge be the characteristic qualities of the rational man, then the American has far less capacity for deliberately organised life than the Englishman or the German.

Among the other paradoxes of the American race—a paradox noted by innumerable observers, is the relation between general intelligence and exceptional talent. It has always

been taken for granted that the higher the level of intelligence within a community, the more frequent will be the
manifestations of talent or genius. But the Americans seem
to us at once the most intelligent and the least intellectual
of white races. You seldom come across the stolid dullness
and vacuous prejudices of the common run of Englishmen
or Germans. The most commonplace American is alert, in-
quisitive, sensitive to criticism, and superficially responsive
to new ideas. The conductor of a car, the chambermaid at an
hotel, the driver of a team, or even the ordinary office clerk,
are nearly always good company: they have heard tell about
most things, they are quick at answering your points, they
are able to accept and put into its place any fact or argument
you may give them. But if an illiterate or dullard or vulgar
fellow is rare among native Americans, so are men and
women of eminent distinction. This is all the more surprising
since you are always meeting persons *who look distinguished;*
men with shapely foreheads, finely chiselled features, keen
piercing eyes and faces apparently lined with thought;
women who have variety of expression and charm of gesture
which would denote with us mother wit or emotional experience. But directly these attractive beings begin to talk
you find yourself listening to a "brightness" which is not
wit, to sympathetic expressions which fail to be understanding, and to the same old banal assumptions and mediocre
observations, repeated with uniform emphasis but without
conviction—a sort of mechanical repetition of what they have
been hearing all their lives. The tyranny of the stale platitude
is maddening in the U.S.A. There are, of course, in Boston,
New York and Washington, cultivated men of letters, organ-
isers in the business and political world, of high courage and
astonishing shrewdness; laborious students, ingenious in-
ventors, clever and learned lawyers; it might even be urged
that in the brainworking professions there is a higher degree
of competency among the rank and file in America than in
Great Britain, France or Germany. And yet even Americans

admit that in this and the last generation there have appeared in their country no men or women in any way comparable in mental force or originality to a Bismarck, a Renan or a Darwin. There is in fact a dearth of persons at all equal in these respects to the hosts of literary men, scholars, statesmen, artists, scientific men, turned out year by year by the three great European races.

An amazing diversity alike in the origin of the American people and in its physical environment has, in fact, produced a race positively wearisome to the European in the uniformity of its social habits and intellectual assumptions.

About the diversity of origin and physical environment there can be no doubt. Even to-day the traveller sees in the streets of New York, or for that matter of any American city, every imaginable race and type of human being, from the Chinaman, the Japanese and the black man, to the American aristocrat of French or Dutch descent, the New England descendant of the eighteenth century Englishman and the Jewish financier with a German name. In this vast continent there is every variety in climate, scenery and natural resources: rocky mountains, rolling plains, extreme fertility and irredeemable barrenness; arctic cold and tropical heat, products ranging from fur to cotton, from coal to gold—a physical environment in fact so extraordinarily diverse that the modern believer in functional adaptation would have confidently predicted that even if the continent had been peopled simultaneously by one race, with one creed and one tradition—half a dozen distinct and separate civilisations would have sprung up in this wonderful new world. And yet in associating with the citizens of New York or Denver, of Washington or Chicago, the traveller discovers the same daily life, the same impelling motives, the same root principles, the same assumptions and implications as to what is ultimately expedient and desirable in personal life, in social relations and in the government of the country. Whether you attend the meetings of a great Eastern municipality or those of a

Western State Legislature, whether you observe the procedure of the Federal Congress or that of a Board of Supervisors of a mining camp, you discover exactly the same devices—the same sort of standing orders for instance—the
same conceptions of the relation of the representative to the
constituencies or to the officials, the same controversies,
though possibly in different stages of development; fre-
quently the same desire for a new constitution of exactly the
same pattern.

Now I cannot believe that this absence of distinguished
talent and of variety of type is a necessary characteristic of
the American race. For even if the native born Americans
of American parentage inherited this lack of genius and uniformity of type, the barrenness of the foreign born has still
to be accounted for. There seems better logic and more charity in the hypothesis that there is something in the way of
life and the mental environment of the U.S.A. that hinders
or damps down the emergence of intellectual or artistic distinction. If I were to give myself away by trying to account
for this unverified fact (?) I should trace it largely to two
radically false assumptions with which all Americans start
on their career—assumptions which are now so deeply
rooted in their social life and political constitution that all
contrary views are strangled long before they get hold of a
sufficient body of people to alter the mental environment of
the next generations. Further, these fallacies are so agreeable
to the ordinary man that they are at once accepted by every
immigrant as the necessary basis of free institutions.

The first of these fallacies is the old constitutional maxim
that "all men are born free and equal;" with its derivative
that one man is as good as another and equally fitted to deliver judgment on every conceivable question. "Our fore-
fathers" pleaded Samuel Adams in 1776 "threw off the yoke
of Popery and religion; for you is reserved the honour of
levelling the popery of politics; they opened the Bible to all
and maintained the capacity of every man to judge for him-

self in religion. Are we sufficient for the comprehension of the sublimest truths, and unequal to material and temporal ones?" It is this Protestantism, it is this assumption that there is no such thing as the expert, and that all men are equally good judges in all questions, that is one of the fallacies that eats away the roots of any American genius by blinding his fellow citizens to his peculiar talent or attainments. The common run of Americans object to any pretention to a higher standard of intelligence, or any assertion of an original point of view as a direct denial of the basis of American democracy. Thus the stronger and more original mind is robbed of its freedom and its self-confidence. The man of real originality of outlook or intensity of talent cannot rise to be the leader of his fellows. Some Englishmen thank their luck as a nation, that the old attitude of reverence to kings, nobles, priests, has been gradually transferred to men of distinction during the transitional years from political oligarchy to political democracy. The Englishman, they say, has inherited sufficient experience of affairs to reject the rotten metaphysics of Protestantism and to perceive that the whole modern theory of division of labour leads straight to increased specialisation of particular faculties in particular people, and to the careful selection of experts for the finer work of a complicated civilisation.

The second assumption is perhaps less consciously held, but is more universally acted upon. It is the old fallacy of the classic economists that each man will best serve the interests of the whole community by pursuing his own gain. It is interesting to note that this axiom was invented by English thinkers; but it has never been fully accepted by the English people. We have always, for instance, excluded this motive from our conception of public affairs. No Englishman ever imagines that the government of the Empire can be run on the principle of each official seeking his own pecuniary interests. On the contrary, it is assumed that all public men, from the Prime Minister to the humblest civil servant, will spend his energies on the performance of the service for which he is paid, and not on increasing his income. Likewise, whole classes in England have vigourously rejected this maxim. Even our landed aristocracy who are dominated by class interest and believe that their ownership of the land leads to the best of all possible worlds, habitually, when they hold public office, subordinate their personal if not their class interest to what they conceive to be the welfare of the nation. And our working men, as a class, have throughout asserted in the teeth of the economists and of their capitalist employers, that if each manual worker attempts to gain the largest wage with the least friction, the whole class of manual workers will suffer in prosperity and the nation itself decline in riches. Americans on the other hand, of whatever class, and of all occupations, accept pecuniary self-interest as the one and only propelling motive, and are almost ashamed to admit that they are inspired by any other. Even in the exceptional case of a man becoming obsessed by the success of the institution which he manages, it is with the *pecuniary* position of the institution that he is most concerned. The Presidents of Universities, the Ministers of Churches, are all out for money. "If you talk like that" said an American Bishop to a newly arrived Anglican priest who had been boldly asserting the responsibilities of wealth "you will never see that church of yours rebuilt. You had better give up these theories of yours and attend to your own business." All professions, all occupations, resolve themselves into a race for money. However diverse may be the origin and physical environment of a people, if they have but one motive there can be but one faculty. Hence the all-pervading and all-devouring "executive" capacity of the American people.

The levelling down of all intellectual eminence is not the worst result of these two fallacies. This unlucky combination of intellectual Protestantism, with an overpowering faith in the moral validity of pecuniary self-interest accounts for the misgovernment of the American people. In the U.S.A. we watch a great aggregate of men and women, individually endowed with courage, humane feeling, self-control and mental energy, who nevertheless in association with each other produce a Government which is at once sordid and shallow, corrupt and inefficient. For who can deny the truth of Professor Bryce's remark that for the last twenty years the Federal Congress had shirked every problem and evaded every issue. Who can watch the proceedings of the Senate or of the House at the present time without noticing the absence of any straightforward leadership, and the presence of a subterranean government carried on in the interests of small groups of profitmakers and without any consideration of the interests of the whole people. And the defects of the Federal Government, its lack of moral dignity and intellectual activity, its subordination to underground financial corruption and the irresponsible screechings of sensational journalism, are completely outdone by the open thefts and glaring incompetence of the municipal authorities, large and small, in every district and every state. The School Boards practically are bought by the School Book Trust, the County Assessors lower the valuation of the property of privileged persons until the wealthy man almost escapes taxation. And if you ask the well-to-do American why all this corruption is allowed to happen, he tells you quite frankly that representatives and senators do not go to Washington or the State capital "for their health" and that he supposes they must be allowed to make something out of it. Or a leading lawyer like Greenleaf Thompson explains at great length that the popular government of cities must necessarily resolve itself into government by syndicates, and that the spoils system is fully justified on sound individualist principles. Still deeper down in the heart of every free-born American is the conviction that Government is an easy matter for which one man is as good as another and that therefore political parties are justified in putting into any office their political workers. Even the reformers seem contaminated with one

or other of these fallacies and you find an earnest and powerful politician like ex-Governor Altgeld insisting that the
cure for all evils in Federal, State and Municipal Government
is a clause in all constitutions making all officials ineligible
for re-election after a short term of office, whilst the Mug
Wumps are perpetually assuring you that municipalities must
be run on "business principles" quite forgetting that business
is run for the profit of the people who control it, which is
exactly the cause of the corrupt American municipality. No-
one in America seems to realise that good government rests
not merely on democratic institutions but on the growth of a
new motive, that of social service combined with the selection of men for the work of government according to their
capacity for that work.[9]

9. Sidney Webb refrained from the ambitious generalizations about the
United States that his wife undertook, but in a letter from Australia to his
friend and colleague Graham Wallas he did offer one political generalization:
"Australia is utterly and completely unlike America in every respect. From
top to bottom there is absolutely no likeness or analogy. So whatever dis-
couragement you derived from America—in the quite unfounded belief that
the U.S. is a Democratic country—this place would restore your spirits, and
persuade you that what is wrong in the U.S. is the peculiar copy of 18th
century Toryism that Hamilton fastened on America 120 years ago. Not that
this place is 'advanced'—it is very much what England was in 1870" (Sidney
Webb to Graham Wallas, Melbourne, Australia, October 20, 1898).

([*Honolulu*
July 15th 1898

Our voyage across the Pacific Ocean was a contrast
in every way from our disagreeable encounter with the
Atlantic. Instead of a floating hotel, in which the saloon passengers are confined strictly to the central platform of the
upper deck, we were on a real living ship, with a bow and
a stern accessible, so that we could commune alone with the
waves, and yet big enough to avoid the sensation of being
couped in a mere boat on the waters. The captain and the
passengers were homely folk—the former not standing on his
dignity like Captain Cameron, the latter not "stinking of
money" like the passengers on board the White Star "Teu-
tonic". But beyond all these better circumstances there was
a calm, mystically blue ocean, with a placid surface, sometimes reflecting the flight of the black seagulls, at others
breaking into bright sparkling little waves, flying fish dashing from one end to the other. At meal times we chatted to
the Captain and a well-bred English China merchant: between whiles we smoked, read and wrote. I began an elab-

orate "Reflections" on America and got entangled in an attempt to make it readable—the last pages of my MSS. book becoming a marvellous network of corrections.

On the 13th we sailed into Honolulu harbour: our deck railings draped with the English and American ensigns, our rigging dressed with flags and the momentous signals "Hawaii annexed to the United States: The Whole Spanish Fleet Sunk off Santyago" flying from our top-masts. An American monitor, lying with steam up, saluted us and sent a boat for mails steaming out for Manilla directly these were received. The soldiers on an American transport lined its rigging and gave us a tremendous ovation—guns were fired from the Executive Buildings, flags went up in all directions, and a crowd of enthusiastic Americans greeted us with cheers and patriotic songs as we were hauled to the landing stage. "Must play to the gallery" whispered our English captain to the English merchant. "It is characteristic that these Americans never remember that they were two to one when they sunk the Spanish fleet." "I wonder what the natives have to say about this 'annexation' of their property—those on the quay look sad or indifferent" remarked the China merchant, with his soft English drawl which brought back the vision of Pall Mall athwart the brilliant sight of the tropical island port. "Is it not enchanting? It is more beautiful than I expected" enthusiastically exclaimed Trevelyan. "The island of Skye, with Kew Gardens let loose on its beach and the temperature of a hot house" irreverently observed Sidney. But now the crowd on the wharf had surged up on to the decks and were warmly greeting or eagerly questioning the passengers and the officers:—four American reporters—our fellow passengers—were distributing copies of their "organs" to clamouring groups: slim Chinese boys were gliding down the gangway with passengers' hand luggage, stalwart natives were handling the heavy trunks as they slid down the wharf; drivers of all nationalities were bargaining with tourists over fares, whilst native children were displaying their prowess as swimmers and divers, doing their little utmost to beguile you into throwing small change into the deep transparent water. "Need not wait for your baggage: I'll see it through the custom house" politely urged the hotel porter. Dusty and hot we tramped up the street behind a crowd and the military band, and were soon seated on the verandah of a pleasantly built wooden building surrounded by a garden of palms, tree ferns, flame of the forest, and other wondrously formed foliage—enjoying the new sensation of being in the tropics—a sensation somewhat damped by the strains of the "Star Spangled Banner" and the firing off of the inevitable American crackers! [10]

We are not here to investigate, it is far too hot—too persistently hot night and day. Surf-riding and bathing with the charming Princess Kaiulani—the niece and heir apparent of the Ex-Queen—is far more attractive than cross-examining the respectable non-conformist deacons, who, in a double capacity, make up the annexed Government and represent the annexing Government. The tale seems somewhat of this sort: [Until] 1873 heaven favoured Hawaii with a succession of native Kings who were wise in their generation. They kept their native subjects happy with plots of land and frequent revivalist services, whilst permitting the shrewd Yankee missionaries, under the forms of a constitutional monarchy, to govern the Islands, knowing full well that so long as the missionaries were allowed to boss the show, not one of the

10. Mrs. Webb wrote her sister: "We arrived here in fine style—with flying colours, signaling to the expectant inhabitants the Annexation of the Islands to the United States. We were therefore accorded, by the crowd of American settlers gathered at the quay, a magnificent reception—military band, floral wreaths, and the firing of cannon from the Executive buildings. . . . We find the little place in an uproar of excitement. The self-styled oligarchy of respectable American capitalists and lawyers who have been governing since 1893 are in [a] triumphant mood. With a handful of supporters they have been sitting tight on some 115000 inhabitants of all races (and about 6,000 Europeans and Americans) and have never known from day to day whether there might not be a successful conclusion: unsuccessful 'conspiracies' have been a monthly occurrence" (Beatrice Webb to Kate Courtney, Honolulu, July 17, 1898).

Great Powers would be accepted as Sovereign of their Island
Kingdom. It is amusing to read in the local histories how
these pious gentlemen played off Great Britain against
France, Germany against Japan, and the U.S.A. against Europe and Japan alike, and held all these Great Powers at
arms length. But sad to relate, these great native chiefs, af-
flicted with the national malady of barrenness, died without
issue and the Crown was left to be hustled for by the inferior
chiefs in the lobbies of the Legislature. An elected King is
a poor thing at the best; and in this case the choice went
from bad to worse, until a queen arrived who thought she
would govern as well as reign, and pressed on the ministers
a brand new autocratic constitution. Or, as another version
runs, the American Consul, thinking that the day had come
for a step forward, landed a company of marines from the
United States battle ship "Boston," on the pretext that American lives and American property were endangered by a
Royal *coup d'etat*. Anyway, the sons of the aforesaid missionaries, who had, as the British resident told us, given up
religion and taken to real estate, found themselves sitting,
one morning early in the year of our Lord 1893, as a provisional government in the Royal Palace, the Queen having
been quietly moved in the night to one of her villas well
within reach of the guns of the "Boston." The provisional
government forthwith proceeded to nominate a convention
to draft a constitution for the New Republic. (For this constitution see our American documents). For the next five
years the Islands were governed by a knot of sensible American business men—biassed in favour of their own race and
their own class—but apparently honest enough and quite
decently efficient. Meanwhile a potent economic interest was
making for annexation by the United States. Thick patches
of waving sugar cane, increasing in length and depth year
by year were creeping round the Island. Money was being
made, hand over hand, the greed of riches grew apace. An-

nexation by the United States of America would mean untold millions in the pockets of the resident capitalists, by ridding them of the United States import duty on refined sugar. Once this was got rid of, monster refineries would rise up and tower over the waving sugar cane, and the Hawaiian sugar planter could snap his fingers at the Sugar Trust, or come into it on his own terms. Moreover, sitting tight on 150,000 unrepresented Chinese and Japanese labourers and petty traders disfranchised on account of alien race, still more on the native Hawaiians who refused to recognise the Republic, out of a total population of 120,000 was not a comfortable state of being. The little oligarchy of American business men found they were sufficiently occupied in economic exploitation without undertaking the task of political government. So deputations were sent to Washington to plead for annexation: each new conspiracy discovered among the Hawaiians and half Whites, each new exaction of the Sugar Trust increasing the fervency of the appeal. But all in vain. On the refusal to annex Hawaii, President Cleveland and Speaker Reed were agreed, and neither the Democratic nor the Republican Party was allowed to take the matter up. Then came the war, with the sinking of Spanish fleets, with Dewey's, Hobson's and Sampson's exploits, with martial glory and worldwide Empire written large in the headlines of every newspaper, and the whole American people carried away by childish delight in its new militarism. And so we sailed into Honolulu on the 13th day of July 1898 with ship dressed and signal flying "Hawaii annexed to the United States" "Must play to the gallery" said the English captain.

¶*July 20th.*
Our six days have passed pleasantly. "Good Society" in Honolulu consists of the immediate descendants of the missionaries—Judds, Castles, Doles, Armstrongs, McGraws; and of the Royalist set, centring round the charming Kaiulani.

We had introductions to both these ruling factions—though, for that matter, an introduction to either would have sufficed, since political bitterness has not produced any hard and fast social cleavage. There are many houses in which annexationists and Royalists meet. The "missionaries" have long since ceased "to mission:" they are the substantial men of business, the leading lawyers and directors of the place; they have been from the beginning connected with the Government; Old Dr. [Gerrit Parmele] Judd, the father of the present Chief Justice, being the statesman who saved Hawaiian independence and secured the good will of Europe and the U.S.A. To-day they are the provisional government. It remains to be seen whether an incoming Party machine will oust these old settlers from their political domain. Mostly of New England stock, they are sturdy self-controlled persons, puritans in temper and in conduct. But here arises a humourous situation. For the last fifty years these New England puritans have been closely connected with a Court which, though nominally Christian, was always breaking out into Heathen orgies, and with a race whose charming manners and delightful good temper completely fails to hide an ever-present and urgent lasciviousness. So the children of the Pilgrim Fathers in Hawaii, having extended their knowledge of human beings and got rid of most of their theology, are to-day about as hard-headedly tolerant as the most blasé diplomats in Europe. Staid looking dames, with the slender figures, delicate features and refined expressions of the most correct New Englander, will discuss pleasantly together who may be the father of some aristocratic Hawaiian or leading half-white and will calmly proceed to attribute the children of one of their women friends to different men of their acquaintance. As yet they are not themselves contaminated, except perhaps in the matter of scandalous gossip in which all Honolulu society delights.

The princess is a pathetic figure—an attractive graceful

creature, a mermaid in the water and a great lady out of it. Well-educated, with a romantic feeling towards her mother's people and a natural attraction to the more complicated civ- ilisation of Europeans, intensely conscious alike of her "roy- alty" and of the blood of a beaten and barbaric race, she starts life a strained and forlorn creature. She now lives with her "legal" father, a Scotch merchant who recently failed in business. And hereby hangs a tale of the scandalous charac- ter that Honolulu society delights in. The late King married his sister to this Mr. Cleghorn for reasons of his own and against the lady's inclination, who favoured a Hawaiian. As Cleghorn was a dissipated man with mistresses and children, and as the princess had the promiscuous tendencies of her race, the two led an indescribable life: some of the more re- spectable of the illegitimate daughters leaving the house as too disreputable. After many years without children Kaiulani appeared, reputed the daughter of an American naval officer. An English friend of the family took pity on this child and sent her to school in England, a circumstance which cost her the reversion of the throne, for the American revolutionists would not accept her as Regent since they feared the English influence around her. Now she is back in Honolulu, living among the palms and in the sea, with a pretty friendship growing up between her and an attractive New Englander, Andrew Adams, a tall, slight, chiselled featured young fel- low with a bright intelligence and romantically chivalrous disposition. But he is poor and proud, and she is rich and ambitious; otherwise one would hope for the fit ending to the whole story: the successful wooing of the last of the Ha- waiian chiefs by the typical New England puritan.

I can imagine settling down here for a year to investigate the characteristics of the three races—Hawaiians, Chinese and Japanese—and their quite innumerable crosses. No one here seems to have had the energy to make a careful investi- gation of these different races, and the results of their intermarrying. The Hawaiians and the Chinese are amazingly complementary in characteristics: the Hawaiians sympathetic, musical, intensely amorous and incurably idle; the Chinese deliberate, silent, uncannily industrious, cautious in self-indulgence, careful of their families, and intensely acquisitive, but apparently without imagination and completely absorbed in routine and mechanical work for profit. The Hawaiians are barren, some observers ascribing this barrenness to the ravages of syphilis and promiscuous intercourse, others again to the fatalism which has taken possession of the race—a conviction that they are doomed. Whatever may be the cause, the women are especially skilled in abortion.

The Chinese are great favourites with the ruling class of the ruling race. They make excellent servants: obedient, industrious, clean and silent. Washing-bills are about a quarter as much as in the United States owing to the presence of the Chinese. Then again they pay munificent rents for their rice-plots: £6 a year for an acre; they work far into the night standing knee deep in water. This gains them the good word of these sons of missionaries who have taken to real estate. It would be an interesting enquiry as to the relative rent producing faculty of various races, and what relation this rent producing faculty has to the standard of life. Probably the Jew and Chinaman are the most productive of rent to their respective land-owners, seeing that they resemble each other in combining a low standard of life with ambition and persistent industry.

The Japanese are not regarded so favourably by the capitalists. They are usually allowed to be more intelligent and versatile, but they have objectionable notions as to leisure and a quite intolerable personal independence. They have even been suspected of meditating a strike against their labour contracts when annexation is finally declared, believing that the United States law prohibits contract labour. Then they have shown signs of wishing to take part in politics and bitterly resent being excluded from citizenship as Asiatics.

Altogether they are a troublesome element in Honolulu for
the Powers that be. "And with all these pretentions they are
after all mere imitators, they used to imitate the Chinese, now
they imitate us. They have become a nuisance" contemptu-
ously remarked an owner of rice-fields.

(*July 25th. Pacific: just about the Equator.*
. . . We are now five days off Honolulu . . .

BIOGRAPHICAL DIRECTORY

INDEX

⟨BIOGRAPHICAL DIRECTORY

Adams, Alva. 1850–1922. Elected governor of Colorado as Democrat in 1886, as a Democrat and Silver Republican in 1896. Elected governor again in 1904, but his Republican opponent contested the election and took the office. Member of Democratic National Committee in 1908.

Adams, Charles Francis. 1866–1954. Great-grandson of John Quincy Adams. Lawyer and financier. Member of the Quincy City Council, 1893–94, and mayor of Quincy, 1896–97. Secretary of the Navy under Hoover, 1929–33.

Addams, Jane. 1860–1935. Founder of Hull House, Chicago, 1889. One of the founders of the Women's International League for Peace and Freedom.

Allison, William B. 1829–1908. Republican from Iowa. In House of Representatives, 1863–71; elected to Senate, 1872. Bi-metallist co-author of Bland-Allison Act, 1878.

Altgeld, John Peter. 1847–1902. Democratic governor of Illinois, 1892–96. Pardoned the three surviving anarchists who had been convicted after the Haymarket affair of 1887. Opposed President Cleveland's use of the army to quell the American Railway Union strike of 1894.

Ashley, William James. 1860–1927. One of the pioneers of economic history in the English-speaking world. Professor of Political Economy and Constitutional History at University of Toronto, 1888–92; Professor of Economic History at Harvard University, 1892–1901; thereafter Professor of Commerce, University of Birmingham. Author of *An Introduction to English Economic History and Theory* (2 vols., 1888, 1893), *The Economic Organization of England* (1914). Knighted in 1917.

Babcock, Joseph W. 1850–1909. Republican lumberman from Wisconsin. Elected to House of Representatives, 1892, and quickly became prominent on his side of the House. Supported Robert M. La Follette in 1900, but broke with him in 1902 and lost his seat to a La Follette-backed candidate in 1906.

Bacon, Sir Hickman. 1855–1945. Premier baronet of Britain. Large landowner. Interested in the Webbs' projects.

Bailey, Joseph W. 1863–1929. Mississippi-born and reared, elected as Democrat to House of Representatives from Texas in 1890. House minority leader from 1896 until he went to Senate in 1901. Left Senate in 1913. Free silverite and anti-imperialist.

Balfour, Gerald, second Earl of Balfour. 1853–1945. Conservative Member of Parliament for Central Leeds, 1885–1906. Became President of Board of Trade, 1900. Left politics after his defeat in 1906 and engaged in what he called "psychical research," mainly mental telepathy. Married to Lady Elizabeth Edith Bulwer-Lytton.

Beatty, William Henry. (1838–1914). Ohio-born, Virginia-educated lawyer and jurist. Associate Justice of Supreme Court of Nevada, 1875–80. Chief Justice of California Supreme Court, 1888–1914.

Black, Frank S. 1853–1913. Republican governor New York, 1897–99; in House of Representatives one term before becoming governor. Prominent lawyer.

Bradlaugh, Charles. 1833–91. Prominent English freethinker and advocate of birth control. Proprietor of the *National Reformer,* 1862–91. Elected to House of Commons in 1860, he was refused his seat because he would not take an oath on the Bible. Was elected five more times, and after several suits was allowed to take his seat in 1886. Associate of Annie Besant before she became a socialist.

Brooks, John Graham. 1846–1938. Lecturer and author on economics. Graduate of Harvard Divinity School, 1875, and student
in German universities. Instructor in Political Economy at Harvard and Lecturer in University of Chicago Extension Department. Author of *American Syndicalism* (1913).

Bryan, William Jennings. 1860–1925. Democratic candidate for
President, 1896, 1900, and 1908. Secretary of State, 1913–15.
Outstanding orator and leader of agrarian wing of Democratic
party.

Cantor, Jacob Aaron. 1854–1921. Reporter on New York *World*
for several years. In New York State Assembly, 1885–87, in State
Senate, 1887–98, and its president in 1893–94. Elected president
of borough of Manhattan, 1901. In House of Representatives,
1913–15.

Chapman, John Jay. 1862–1933. Essayist. Friend of William James
and other Boston intellectuals. Author of *Emerson and Other
Essays* (1898) and *New Horizons in American Life* (1932).

Choate, Joseph H. 1832–1917. Prominent Republican and constitutional lawyer. Minister to Great Britain, 1899–1905.

Clark, John Bates. 1847–1938. Economist. Professor Political Economy at Carleton College, 1877–81, Smith College, 1882–93, Am-
herst College, 1892–95, Columbia University, 1895–1923. Author
of *The Philosophy of Wealth* (1885), *The Distribution of
Wealth* (1899), *The Control of Trusts* (1901), *Essentials of
Economic Theory* (1907).

Courtney, Kate. 1847–1929. Beatrice Webb's second eldest sister.
Married Leonard Courtney, who later became Lord Courtney of
Penwith and who nearly became speaker of the House of Com-
mons in 1885. Accompanied Beatrice on her trip to the United
States in 1873.

Cox, George B. 1853–1916. Republican boss of Cincinnati. The
son of penniless English immigrants, he entered politics at age
eighteen. At age twenty-four he became a member of the City
Council. Except for becoming state inspector of oil in 1888, he
did not hold public office thereafter but was the head of the Republican organization.

Croker, Richard. 1841–1922. Irish-born Tammany politician.
Entered politics in 1865, having been a machinist. Held various
posts in New York City government. Lived in Ireland, 1907–19.

Davitt, Michael. 1846–1906. Irish revolutionist and labor agitator. Lost his right arm at age twelve when an operative in a Lancashire cotton mill. Although a Fenian in his youth, he later fought for Irish independence by constitutional means. Became influenced by Henry George. Late in life became secular and socialist in outlook. When he supported the Labor party in England in 1906 and urged secular education, the Church closed the Irish press to him.

Dewey, Davis Rich. 1858–1942. Economist. Professor at Massachusetts Institute of Technology, 1893–1933. Author of *Financial History of the United States* (1902, many later revisions).

Drage, Geoffrey. 1860–1955. British shipowner, political figure, writer. Married daughter of Thomas Henry Ismay of the White Star Line. Member of Parliament, 1895–1900. Alderman, London County Council, 1910–19. Writer on labor, sea power, and statistics.

Eliot, Charles W. 1834–1926. President of Harvard University, 1869–1909. Developed the institution from essentially a New England college with attached professional schools to a great university.

Elkins, Stephen Benton. 1841–1911. Secretary of War, United States Senator. Ohio-born and Missouri-reared, he fought in Union army during Civil War. Went to New Mexico territory, where he became a land and mine owner and rose in Republican politics. After railroad building in West Virginia, he became an advisor to Republican Presidential candidate James G. Blaine in 1884. He served as Secretary of War under Benjamin Harrison, 1891–93. Elected to Senate from West Virginia in 1895, where he remained until his death. Co-founder of Davis and Elkins College.

Ely, Richard T. 1854–1943. Economist. Professor Political Economy, University of Wisconsin, 1892–1925. The textbook mentioned in this diary was *Introduction to Political Economy* (1889).

Ford, Worthington Chauncey. 1858–1941. Statistician and historian. Chief of Bureau of Statistics of Department of State, 1885–89, of Department of the Treasury, 1893–1898. Chief, Division of Manuscripts, Library of Congress, 1902–9. Editor, Massachusetts Historical Society, 1909–29. Author of *George Wash-ington* (1899).

Franklin, Fabian. 1853–1939. Hungarian born, was Associate Pro-fessor and Professor of Mathematics, the Johns Hopkins Uni-versity, 1879–95. Editor of *Baltimore News,* 1895–1908, and as-sociate editor of New York *Evening Post,* 1909–17.

Frick, Henry Clay. 1849–1919. Coke and steel manufacturer. As-sociated with Andrew Carnegie until 1899. Primarily respon-sible for the steel company's anti-union policies in the bitter strike of 1892. Later a director of United States Steel Corpora-tion.

Gage, Lyman Judson. 1836–1927. Secretary of Treasury under Wil-liam McKinley and Theodore Roosevelt, 1897–1902. Banker in Chicago, moving to New York after he left Washington.

Gide, Charles. 1847–1932. French economist. Active in the co-op-erative movement, he was an expert on international monetary problems. Best known for *History of Economic Doctrines* (1909), which he wrote with Charles Rist. The textbook men-tioned in this diary was *Principles of Political Economy* (1892).

Gilman, Daniel Coit. 1831–1908. University president. Librarian and Professor of Geography, Yale, 1856–72. President, Univer-sity of California, 1872–75. President of the Johns Hopkins Uni-versity, 1875–1902. President, The Carnegie Institution of Wash-ington, 1902–4. At Johns Hopkins he was instrumental in de-veloping it into the first real American graduate school.

Gorman, Arthur Pue. 1839–1906. Became a protégé of Stephen A. Douglas while a page boy in the House of Representatives. Was Douglas's secretary during the Lincoln-Douglas debates. Be-came president of Chesapeake and Ohio Canal Co., 1872. After serving in Maryland legislature, was elected to U.S. Senate in 1884. Turned the low tariff Wilson bill into the high tariff Wilson-Gorman Act of 1894. Defeated for re-election in 1898, he won election in 1902 and served as Democratic leader until death.

Gould, Elgin R. L. 1860–1915. Canadian-born economist and re-former. Supporter of political aspirations of Seth Low. Served on commission appointed by Governor Charles Evans Hughes, 1907–8, to revise the New York City charter.

Hadley, Arthur T. 1856–1930. Economist. Professor of Political

Science and Political Economy at Yale University, 1886–99. President of Yale, 1899–1921. The textbook mentioned in this diary was *Economics—An Account of the Relations between Private Property and Public Welfare* (1896).

Hanna, Marcus Alonzo. 1837–1904. Ohio capitalist and politician. Successful in coal and iron and transportation, he entered politics and by 1890 was the main power in the Ohio Republican party. Was instrumental in electing William McKinley governor in 1891 and 1893. Chairman of Republican National Committee in 1896. Went to Senate in 1897.

Harper, William Rainey. 1856–1906. Educator and Hebrew scholar. Professor of Semitic Languages at Yale, 1886–92. First president of University of Chicago, 1892–1906.

Hartman, Charles S. 1861–1929. Indiana-born Montana politician and lawyer. Elected to House of Representatives as a Republican in 1892 and 1894 and as a Silver Republican in 1896. He declined the nomination in 1898 and became a Democrat in 1900. Defeated for a House seat on the Democratic ticket, 1910. Minister to Ecuador, 1913–22.

Hill, Ebenezer J. 1845–1917. Canadian-born banker and politician of Norwalk, Connecticut. Served in House of Representatives, 1895–1913, 1915–17.

Hirst, F. W. 1873–1953. English economist and editor. Editor of *The Economist,* 1907–16. Author of *Wall Street and Lombard Street* (1931).

Hoar, George F. 1826–1904. Massachusetts lawyer and Republican politician. Served in House of Representatives, 1869–77, and in the Senate, 1877–1904. An anti-imperialist.

Hobart, Garret A. 1844–99. McKinley's Vice-President. Died in office. Had not held office outside New Jersey until he became Vice-President.

Hollander, Jacob H. 1871–1940. Professor of Finance and Political Economy, Johns Hopkins. Specialist in taxation and public finance.

Holt, Robert Durning. 1832–1908. English shipowner and benefactor of University of Liverpool. Married Laurencina Potter, Beatrice Webb's eldest sister, 1867. Refused a baronetcy.

Ismay, Thomas Henry. 1837–99. English shipowner and capitalist. Acquired the White Star Line, then engaged in Australian shipping, in 1867, and extended its service to regular runs between Liverpool and New York.

Jenks, Jeremiah W. 1856–1929. Michigan-born economist. Ph.D., University of Halle, 1885. Professor of Political Economy, Knox College, 1886–89, Indiana University, 1889–91, Cornell University, 1891–1912, New York University, 1912–29. President of American Economic Association, 1906–7. Author of *The Trust Problem* (1900).

Judd, Gerrit Parmele. 1803–73. Missionary physician in Hawaii. Became advisor to the King and virtual Prime Minister.

Kaiulani (Princess Victoria Kawekiu Kaiulani Cleghorn.) 1875–99. Daughter of A. S. Cleghorn, once governor of Oahu, and Princess Likelike, sister of Queen Liliuokalani. Her mother died young, and she was educated in England. Would have become queen of Hawaii if United States had not annexed the islands.

Laughlin, James Laurence. 1850–1933. Economist. Professor and Head of the Department of Political Economy, University of Chicago, 1892–1916. Editor of *The Journal of Political Economy*, 1892–1933.

Lewis, James Hamilton. 1863–1939. Lawyer and Democratic politician. In House of Representatives from a Seattle district, 1897–99. Defeated candidate for U.S. Senate from Washington, 1899. Moved to Chicago in 1903. Chicago corporation counsel, 1905–7. Unsuccessful race for governor of Illinois, 1908. Elected to U.S. Senate, 1912, defeated for re-election in 1918 and for governor in 1920. Elected to Senate again in 1930, re-elected in 1936.

Lincoln, Robert Todd. 1843–1926. Abraham Lincoln's eldest son. Chicago lawyer. Secretary of War under Presidents Garfield and Arthur, 1881–85. Minister to Great Britain under President Harrison, 1889–93.

Lodge, Henry Cabot. 1850–1924. Historian and Republican politician from Massachusetts. After receiving Ph.D. in history at Harvard University in 1876, he lectured there on American history for three years. In House of Representatives, 1887–93, Senate, 1893–1924. Permanent chairman of Republican national conventions, 1900, 1908, 1920.

Low, Seth. 1850–1916. Municipal reformer and university president. After a brief career in his father's tea and silk importing business, entered reform politics and served two terms as Republican mayor of Brooklyn, 1882–86. As president of Columbia University, 1889–1901, he moved the institution to its present location on Morningside Heights and brought about the affiliation of Barnard College, Teachers College, and the College of Physicians and Surgeons. Defeated in his bid, 1897, to be elected first mayor of Greater New York City. Elected mayor in 1901. Was not re-elected.

Marshall, Alfred. 1842–1924. English economist. Foremost advocate of neoclassical economic theory. Professor at Cambridge, 1885–1908. The textbook mentioned here is *Principles of Economics* (1890).

Mayo-Smith, Richmond. 1854–1901. Professor of Political Economy, Columbia University, 1883–1901. Author of *Statistics and Economics* (1899).

Mead, Edwin Doak. 1849–1937. Editor, reformer, and peace worker. Edited *The New England Magazine,* 1889–1901. Editor of the *Old South Historical Leaflets.*

Mill, John Stuart. 1806–73. English social philosopher and economist. His social outlook approached socialism in his later years. Perhaps best known for his *Essay on Liberty* (1859). A friend of Beatrice Webb's family. The work on economics mentioned in this diary is *Principles of Political Economy* (2 vols., 1848).

Miller, Frank Justus. 1858–1938. Classical scholar and a dean at University of Chicago, 1892–1925.

Mills, Herbert Elmer. Professor of Political Economy, Vassar College. Ph.D., Cornell, 1890.

Mitchell, John T. W. 1828–95. English leader of co-operative movement. Primary founder of Rochdale Co-operative Manufacturing Society.

Morley, John. Viscount Morley of Blackburn. 1838–1923. Author of books on Gladstone, Emerson, Voltaire, Rousseau. Resigned from the Asquith cabinet in 1914 on pacifist grounds. No admirer of the Webbs, he was a friend of Beatrice's sister and brother-in-law, Kate and Leonard Courtney.

Olivier, Sydney. Baron Olivier. 1859–1943. English Fabian and civil servant. Acting Governor and then Governor of Jamaica, 1907–13. Secretary of State for India in the 1924 Labor party government.

Onslow, William H., Fourth Earl of Onslow. 1853–1911. Governor of New Zealand, 1889–92; Undersecretary of State for India, 1895–1900, and for the colonies, 1900–1903; Alderman on London County Council, 1896–99.

Pauncefote, Sir Julian. 1828–1902. British Ambassador to the United States, 1889–1902. A leading figure in bringing about better Anglo-American relations in the late nineteenth century.

Pease, Edward R. 1857–1955. A founder of the Fabian Society, which met in his rooms in its earliest days. Secretary of the Society until his retirement in 1939.

Phelan, James D. 1861–1930. Millionaire Irish-American politician of California. Mayor of San Francisco, 1897–1902. Regent of University of California. Democratic Senator from California, 1915–21.

Platt, Thomas C. 1833–1910. Republican political leader from New York. In House of Representatives, 1873–77. In Senate for two months in 1881, when he resigned over a disagreement about patronage with President Garfield. In Senate again, 1896–1909.

Playne, Mary. 1849–1923. Beatrice Webb's third oldest sister. Married Arthur Playne, a country squire and textile mill owner of Gloucestershire.

Powderly, Terence V. 1849–1924. Grand master workman of the Knights of Labor, 1879–93. Mayor of Scranton, Pennsylvania, 1879–83. U.S. Commissioner General of Immigration, 1897–1902, and Chief of the Division of Information in the Bureau of Immigration, 1907–21.

Quay, Matthew S. 1833–1904. Republican leader of Pennsylvania. Although holding only minor office, he was the primary figure in the GOP in Philadelphia and Pennsylvania in 1870's and 1880's. Served in U.S. Senate, 1887–99. In 1899 the Pennsylvania legislature deadlocked and elected no Senator. When the governor appointed Quay, the Senate refused to seat him. The legislature thereupon elected him to fill the vacancy, and he served in the Senate until his death.

Quincy, Josiah. 1859–1919. Democratic mayor of Boston, 1895–99. In Massachusetts politics his entire career.

Rainsford, William Stephen. 1850–1933. Episcopal clergyman. Rector of St. George's, New York City, 1882–1906, during which tenure he opposed and defeated on a matter of church policy his most powerful parishioner, J. P. Morgan.

Reed, Thomas B. "Czar." 1839–1902. Autocratic Speaker of the

House of Representatives from Maine. Member of Congress, 1877–99. Speaker of 51st, 54th, and 55th Congresses. Resigned in 1899, although re-elected.

Reynolds, James B. 1861–1924. Lawyer and social worker. Board member of the University Settlement, New York City. Seth Low's secretary, 1902–3. Member of Roosevelt's special commission to investigate the Chicago Stock Yards, 1906. Assistant District Attorney of New York County, 1910–13.

Ritchie, Charles Thomson. 1838–1906. Tory politician. Member of Parliament, 1874. Became head of Board of Trade in 1895. As head of the Local Government Board, 1886–92, played a prominent role in the creation of the London County Council.

Schurman, Jacob Gould. 1854–1942. Canadian-born, English- and German-educated professor of philosophy and university president. President of Cornell University, 1892–1920. Minister to China, 1921–25, Ambassador to Germany, 1925–30. Author of *Kantian Ethics and the Ethics of Evolution* (1881) and *The Ethical Import of Darwinism* (1888).

Scott, Francis Markoe. 1848–1922. Lawyer and jurist. Corporation counsel of New York City, 1895–97. Justice of Supreme Court of New York, First District, 1898–1918.

Seligman, E. R. A. 1861–1939. Lecturer or Professor of Political Economy, Columbia University, 1885–1931. Specialist on taxation. Author of *The Economic Interpretation of History* (1902).

Shaw, Albert. 1857–1947. Editor and scholar. Received Ph.D. from the Johns Hopkins University, 1884, one of the first recipients of a doctor's degree from the new American graduate school. Founded *American Review of Reviews* and served as its editor, 1891–1937.

Shaw, George Bernard. 1856–1950. Irish playwright and essayist. An early Fabian. Close friend of Sidney Webb.

Small, Albion W. 1854–1926. Sociologist. In 1892 he founded at the University of Chicago the first department of sociology in the United States.

Stephens, H(enry) Morse. 1857–1919. Scottish-born, English-educated professor of history in American universities. Cornell University, 1894–1902; University of California, 1902–19. President of American Historical Association, 1915.

Strong, William L. 1827–1900. Ohio-born New York merchant and politician. Last mayor of New York before the creation of Greater New York City in 1898.

Trevelyan, Charles Philips. 1870–1958. Eldest son of Sir George Otto Trevelyan, the historian and statesman. Graduate of Harrow and Trinity College, Cambridge. Member of London school board, 1896–97. M.P. for a district in the West Riding, Yorkshire, as a Liberal, 1899–1918, for Central Newcastle as Labor, 1922–31. Held a minor office in the Asquith government but resigned in 1914 on pacifist principles.

Trevelyan, Robert Calverly. 1872–1951. Younger brother of Charles P. Trevelyan. Author of several volumes of poetry.

Van Wyck, Robert Anderson. 1849–1918. New York lawyer and politician. Defeated Seth Low to become first mayor of Greater New York City, 1898.

Von Holst, Hermann Eduard. 1841–1904. Born and educated in Germany. Professor of History at Strassbourg and Freiburg, 1872–92. Professor and Head of the Department of History, University of Chicago, 1892–1904.

Waite, Davis Hanson. 1825–1901. Populist governor of Colorado, 1893–94. Defeated in bid for re-election, 1894. Often called "Bloody Bridles" because of his statement that it would be better "that blood should flow to the horses' bridles rather than our national liberties should be destroyed."

Wald, Lillian D. 1867–1940. Nurse and social worker. Founder in 1893 of the Henry Street Settlement in New York City.

Walker, Francis A. 1840–97. Economist and educator. Professor of Political Economy at Yale, 1873–81. President of the Massachusetts Institute of Technology, 1881–97. The economics text referred to here was *Political Economy* (1883).

Wallas, Graham. 1858–1932. English sociologist. With Webb, Shaw, and Olivier, was one of the "Big Four" of the early Fabian Society. Author of *Human Nature in Politics.*

Ward, Lester Frank. 1841–1913. Geologist and sociologist. With U.S. Geological Survey, 1881–1906. Professor of Sociology, Brown University, 1906–13. Author of *Dynamic Sociology* (1883), *Pure Sociology* (1903).

Warwick, Charles F. 1852–1913. Philadelphia lawyer and politician. District Attorney, Philadelphia County, 1881–84; City Solicitor, 1884–95; Mayor, 1895–99.

Williams, Talcott. 1849–1928. Journalist. With New York *World,* 1873–77. Washington correspondent for New York *Sun* and San Francisco *Chronicle,* 1877–79. Editorial writer for Springfield (Mass.) *Republican,* 1879–81. Same for Philadelphia *Press,* 1881–1912. Director of School of Journalism, Columbia University, 1912–19.

Wolcott, Roger. 1847–1900. Massachusetts lawyer and politician. Lieutenant governor, 1892–96, succeeding to governorship at governor's death in 1896. Elected governor, 1896, 1897, and 1898. Declined to run again. Republican.

Wright, Carroll D. 1840–1909. Statistician. Commissioner of U.S. Bureau of Labor in the Department of the Interior, 1885–1905. First president of Clark College, Worcester, Massachusetts, 1902–9. President of American Statistical Association, 1897–1909.

Zueblin, Charles. 1866–1924. Sociologist. University of Chicago, 1892–1908. Founded Northwestern University Settlement, 1892. Editor, *Twentieth Century Magazine,* 1911–12.

DATE DUE